ASVAB FLASHCARDS

ARMY • AIR FORCE • NAVY • MARINES • COAST GUARD

 TestWare® Edition

Lisa K. Druck

D1018750

 Research & Education Association
Visit our website at: www.rea.com

Research & Education Association
61 Ethel Road West
Piscataway, New Jersey 08854
E-mail: info@rea.com

ASVAB Flashcard Book
With TestWare® on CD-ROM

Published 2013

Printed in the United States of America

ISBN-13: 978-0-7386-0908-9
ISBN-10: 0-7386-0908-0

REA® and TestWare® are registered trademarks of
Research & Education Association, Inc.

C13-0101

From the Author

The ASVAB (Armed Services Vocational Aptitude Battery) is the most important exam you will take in your military career. The scores you receive on the exam's 10 subtests will determine your placement within the U.S. Armed Services.

The exam's 10 subtests are:

- Arithmetic Reasoning (AR)
- Mathematics Knowledge (MK)
- Word Knowledge (WK)
- Paragraph Comprehension (PC)
- General Science (GS)
- Electronics Information (EI)
- Auto Information (AI)
- Shop Information (SI)
- Mechanical Comprehension (MC)
- Assembling Objects (AO)

In all likelihood, you are already feeling some level of anxiety regarding the exam, but you can rely on this Flashcard Book to help a great deal.

Not everyone approaches learning or test taking in the same way, but all students and test takers can benefit from using flashcards. This innovative book design—unique to REA—allows you to review each question and its answer choices and then check for the correct answer on the flip side of the card.

Because this Flashcard Book is divided into sections that match the exam's actual subtests you can spend as much time you need on each one. For example, if you are great at putting parts together, you may only need a half hour to brush up on Assembling Objects. However, if vocabulary is not your strong suit, you may need to spend several hours working on Word Knowledge questions. This book will accommodate your learning style and studying needs, and it is sure to help you boost your confidence—and thereby, your scores!

No doubt, some of the subjects will cause you to feel more concern regarding your test performance than others. Rest assured that no matter what your reservations about test taking might be, this Flashcard Book will help build your confidence and enable you to achieve a higher score. By the time you finish using this book, you will be relaxed, self-confident and properly prepared for exam day. As you well know, stability, preparation and self-confidence are key to success . . . and there are no substitutes for them.

This Flashcard Book also contains REA's exclusive TestWare® on CD, which features 100 questions from the book. Take the practice questions on the computer, in randomized order, and get instant scoring. In a flash, you'll know exactly what you need to study the most.

As you can see, this Flashcard Book has everything you need to succeed on the ASVAB: it is jam-packed with information; it is organized to help you study more effectively; it is designed to help you test yourself, in an honest and stress-free manner; it is lightweight and easy to use wherever you want to study.

Most important of all, we honor you for your commitment to serving our country and in so doing, ensuring all the freedoms we cherish. Best of luck in your preparation for the ASVAB and throughout your career in the U.S. military.

Lisa K. Drucker

Table of Contents

About Research & Education Association

Founded in 1959, Research & Education Association (REA) is dedicated to publishing the finest and most effective educational materials—including software, study guides, and test preps—for students in elementary school, middle school, high school, college, graduate school, and beyond.

Today, REA's wide-ranging catalog is a leading resource for teachers, students, and professionals.

We invite you to visit us at *www.rea.com* to find out how "REA is making the world smarter."

Acknowledgments

In addition to the author, we would like to thank Pam Weston, Publisher, for setting the quality standards for production integrity and managing the publication to completion; Larry B. Kling, Vice President, Editorial, for his overall direction; Michael Reynolds, Managing Editor, for project management; and S4Carlisle for typesetting this edition.

CAT-ASVAB
(Computer-adaptive test)

10 SUBTESTS	DESCRIPTION
General Science (GS)	Measures knowledge of life science, earth and space science, and physical science.
Arithmetic Reasoning (AR)	Measures ability to solve basic math problems.
Word Knowledge (WK)	Measures ability to understand the meaning of words through synonyms.
Paragraph Comprehension (PC)	Measures ability to obtain information from written materials.
Mathematics Knowledge (MK)	Measures knowledge of mathematical concepts and applications.
Electronics Information (EI)	Measures knowledge of electrical current, circuits, devices, and electronic systems.
Auto Information (AI)	Measures knowledge of automotive maintenance and repair.
Shop Information (SI)	Measures knowledge of wood and metal shop practices.
Mechanical Comprehension (MC)	Measures knowledge of the principles of mechanical devices, structural support, and properties of materials.
Assembling Objects (AO)	Measures spatial and problem-solving activities.

QUESTIONS

Q–1

A physician advises a patient to take a two-pill dosage of an over-the-counter fever reducer every 3 hours. If the patient follows these instructions and has a bottle containing 160 pills, how many days before the patient will have to buy more of the fever reducer?

(A) 8

(B) 20

(C) 10

(D) 24

Your Answer _____

_____

Q–2

Cpl. Johnson is nervous about her upcoming qualifying exam. In order to pass the test, she must answer 35 out of 50 questions correctly. Represented as a percentage, what minimum grade does she need to get on the test in order to pass?

(A) 75%

(B) 70%

(C) 65%

(D) 80%

Your Answer _____

_____

ANSWERS

A–1

(C) To obtain the correct answer, 10 days, divide the number of hours in a day by the number of times the medication is to be taken each day: $24 \div 3 = 8$. Multiply that number by the amount of pills per dosage to determine the amount of pills taken each day: $8 \times 2 = 16$. The total number of pills in the bottle is 160. Divide that number by the number of pills taken each day: $160 \div 16 = 10$ (choice C).

A–2

(B) Divide 35 by 50 to get .7, then multiply by 100 to get 70% (choice B). Do not be fooled by the fact that 65% is frequently a passing grade! The other choices are incorrect.

QUESTIONS

Q–3

A cosmetics representative travels 800 miles during a 36-hour workweek. If she spends 1/4 of her time on the road visiting customers, how many hours per workweek does she spend in the office?

(A) 9

(B) 10

(C) 30

(D) 27

Your Answer _____

Q–4

Sgt. Walker has put Pfcs. Davis and Hathaway on a road crew. They need 15 buckets of tar for 3/4 mile of road. How many buckets will they need for 4¼ miles?

(A) 85

(B) 65

(C) 45

(D) 60

Your Answer _____

ANSWERS

A–3

(D) The number of miles traveled is not needed to solve the problem. Multiply 36 by 0.75 (3/4) to get 27 (choice D). Make sure to read the question carefully, noting that the answer sought is the number of hours in the office, not the number of hours traveling, which would be 9: 1/4, or 25%, of 36. The other two choices are based on 1/4 and 3/4 of the more common 40-hour workweek and so are incorrect.

A–4

(A) 15 buckets for 3/4 mile means 5 buckets per 1/4 mile. 4¼ miles = 17/4 miles. 17 × 5 = 85. So, 85 buckets will be needed to tar 4¼ miles (choice A). The other choices are incorrect.

QUESTIONS

Q-5

If 6 pairs of shoes and 4 pairs of sneakers cost $230.00, and each pair of shoes costs $25.00, how much does each pair of sneakers cost?

(A) $15.00

(B) $10.00

(C) $5.00

(D) $20.00

Your Answer _____

_____

Q-6

The scale on a map is 1" to 200 miles. On the map, City A is 3¼" from City B. How many actual miles apart are the cities?

(A) 3.25 miles

(B) 6.5 miles

(C) 650 miles

(D) 615 miles

Your Answer _____

_____

ANSWERS

A–5

(D) Find the cost of 6 pairs of shoes: $6 \times 25 = 150$. Find the cost of the sneakers: $230 - 150 = 80$. Find the cost of 1 pair of sneakers: $80 \div 4 = 20$. The correct answer is D. The other choices are incorrect.

A–6

(C) If $1'' = 200$ miles, then $3\frac{1}{4}'' = 3\frac{1}{4} \times 200$. $13/4 \times 200/1 = 2,600 \div 4 = 650$. Do not be fooled by choice A, which is the decimal form of the inch scale given in the question. The correct answer is C.

QUESTIONS

Q-7

The perimeter of a rectangle is 60′. If the length is 20′6″, what is the width of the rectangle?

(A) 10′

(B) 9′6″

(C) 10′6″

(D) 6′6″

Your Answer _____

_____

Q-8

At the PX, a gallon of a sports drink costs $4.96. What is the cost of 2 pints?

(A) $0.62

(B) $2.48

(C) $1.24

(D) $0.31

Your Answer _____

_____

ANSWERS

A–7

(B) The perimeter of a rectangle is equal to the sum of two lengths and two widths. If 1 length equal 20′6″ (20½′), then: 2 × 20½ = 41 (2 lengths). 60 (perimeter) − 41 (2 lengths) = 19 (2 widths): 19 ÷ 2 = 9½′ (1 width). It is easier to calculate the answer with a simple fraction like 1/2 (foot) than 6 (inches). Remember that the answer choices are in inches, so you need to convert from feet back to inches before selecting the answer choice. The correct answer is B.

A–8

(C) Find the cost of 1 pint (1 gallon = 8 pints): 4.96 ÷ 8 = 0.62. Next, find the cost of 2 pints: 2 × 0.62 = 1.24. Be sure to become familiar with basic measurements prior to test day. The correct answer is C.

QUESTIONS

Q–9

A woman left $90,000.00 to her sister and niece. The ratio of the sister's share to the niece's share was 6:4. How much did the niece receive?

(A) $36,000.00

(B) $54,000.00

(C) $22,500.00

(D) $15,000.00

Your Answer _____

Q–10

The grocery manager in a supermarket orders cans of condensed milk by the gross. If he sells 8 cans a day, how many days will it take for the store to go through a gross?

(A) 12 days

(B) 48 days

(C) 18 days

(D) 144 days

Your Answer _____

9

ANSWERS

A–9

(A) Set up an equation where x equals 1 share of $90,000.00. According to the ratio, the sister was left 6 shares ($6x$), and the niece was left 4 shares ($4x$). So, the equation can be written: $6x + 4x = 90,000$. Solve for x by combining like terms: $10x = 90,000$. So, $x = 9,000$. Therefore, 1 share (x) is $9,000.00. Multiply the value of 1 share by the number of shares the niece received: $4x = 36,000$. The niece received $36,000.00. Any time there is a ratio in a question, you will need to set up an equation. Do not be fooled by answer choices that simply divide the amount in the question by the numbers in the ratio, as in choices C and D. And read the choices carefully—choice B is the amount that the sister would receive ($6 \times 9,000 = 54,000$), but the question asks for the amount the niece would receive. The correct answer is A.

A–10

(C) A gross $= 144$. Divide that by the number of items sold per day: $144 \div 8 = 18$ (choice C). Be sure to familiarize yourself with common arithmetic terms like *gross,* as these appear frequently on the exam.

QUESTIONS

Q–11

Lt. Farquhar and her husband are shopping for furniture for their new apartment off base. A sofa that they like usually sells for $600.00, but as thanks for her service to our country, the store owner says they can have it for $525.00. What is the percentage of reduction?

(A) 25%

(B) 75%

(C) 12½%

(D) 8%

Your Answer _____

Q–12

Mr. Blackwell has a life insurance policy with a face value of $20,000.00. At his age (45), the annual premium is $30.00 per $1,000.00. What is the total premium paid for this policy every 3 months?

(A) $150.00

(B) $200.00

(C) $600.00

(D) $1,200.00

Your Answer _____

ANSWERS

A–11

(C) Find the amount of the price reduction by subtracting: $600 - 525 = 75$. To find the percentage of the reduction, divide the reduction amount by the original price: $75 \div 600 = 1/8 = 12\frac{1}{2}\%$. Remember to read the question carefully; $75 = 1/8$ of 600, not 8% (which would be 8/100). The correct answer is C.

A–12

(A) There are 20 units of $1,000.00: $20 \times 30 = 600$, which is the total amount of the premium for 12 months. Divide by 4 in order to determine how much is paid every 3 months: $\$600 \div 4 = 150$. Note that Mr. Blackwell's age, 45, does not need to be used to determine the answer. The correct answer is A.

QUESTIONS

Q–13

A DVD player priced at $500.00 was reduced 20% during a Labor Day sale. There was an additional 15% discount for customers paying cash. What was the cash price of the DVD player during the sale?

(A) $400.00

(B) $425.00

(C) $325.00

(D) $340.00

Your Answer _____

Q–14

Two seamen are required to bring the admiral's car when they get into port. They drive for 8 hours at a speed of 65 miles per hour. If the car covers 26 miles for every gallon of gas used, how many gallons did they use?

(A) 26

(B) 20

(C) 30

(D) 34

Your Answer _____

ANSWERS

A–13

(D) Find the 20% reduction (20% = 1/5): 500 × 1/5 = $100. 500 − 100 = 400. Now find the 15% additional reduction for paying cash: 400 × 0.15 = 60. 400 − 60 = 340. When there are multiple discounts, remember to take the additional discount off the already discounted price; do not add the percentage discounts together and take them both off the original price. The correct answer is D.

A–14

(B) Multiply the hours by the miles per hour to determine the distance they drove: 65 × 8 = 520. Divide the distance by the miles per gallon to determine the number of gallons used: 520 ÷ 26 = 20. The correct answer is B.

QUESTIONS

Q–15

A Memorial Day parade attracted a crowd of 1,500 people; 30% were children. How many adults came to the parade?

(A) 1,050

(B) 1,000

(C) 500

(D) 450

Your Answer _____

_____

Q–16

An order-entry clerk earns $9.50 per hour. If she works from 8 A.M. until 5:30 P.M. with a half hour for lunch, how much does she earn in one workday?

(A) $81.00

(B) $80.75

(C) $85.50

(D) $76.00

Your Answer _____

_____

ANSWERS

A–15

(A) If 30% were children, 70% were adults (0.7). Multiply that by the number of the total crowd to get the number of adults: 1,500 × 0.7 = 1,050. Be careful when converting percentages to decimals and fractions. The correct answer is A.

A–16

(C) From 8 A.M. until 5:30 P.M. is 9½ hours, less the half hour for lunch, equals a 9-hour workday. Multiply the work hours by the hourly rate of pay: 9 × $9.50 = $85.50. Use the information given in the question, and always check carefully to make sure that you have included everything you need to solve the problem. The correct answer is C.

QUESTIONS

Q–17

Two planes leave the same Air Force base, traveling in opposite directions. The first plane is flying at the rate of 360 miles per hour; the second plane, at 390 miles per hour. In how many hours will the two planes be 4,500 miles apart?

(A) 5

(B) 8

(C) 6

(D) 7

Your Answer _____

Q–18

Ms. Ambrose invests $5,000.00 at 4% annual interest. How much more must she invest at 5% annual interest in order receive an annual interest of $1,000.00 from both investments?

(A) $5,000.00

(B) $8,000.00

(C) $10,000.00

(D) $16,000.00

Your Answer _____

ANSWERS

A–17

(C) Determine the number of miles apart the planes will be after an hour of travel: 360 + 390 = 750. To determine how many hours it will take for them to be 4,500 miles apart, divide the total miles by the number of miles apart per hour: 4,500 ÷ 750 = 6 (choice C).

A–18

(D) First, determine the interest on the amount invested at 4%: $5,000.00 × 0.40 = $200. Next, determine how much more interest she wants to receive in dollars: $1,000 − $200 = $800. This $800.00 will equal 5% of the additional amount (x) she needs to invest. Set up an equation: $800 = 0.05 × ($x$). To solve for x, divide each side of the equation by 0.05:

$$\frac{800.00}{0.05} = \left(\frac{0.05}{0.05}\right)x$$

$$16,000 = x$$

The amount she needs to invest at 5% interest is $16,000.00 (choice D). Remember to clear the decimal in the divisor to solve the problem.

QUESTIONS

Q–19

Using the following formula, find the value of *C* when
F = 68. *C* = 5/9(*F* − 32).

(A) 20

(B) 38

(C) 36

(D) 180

Your Answer _____

Q–20

The Browns bought an $800.00 electric range marked at a 25% discount. They made a down payment of $150.00 and agreed to pay the balance in 12 equal monthly installments. How much was each installment?

(A) $50.00

(B) $37.50

(C) $67.00

(D) $54.00

Your Answer _____

ANSWERS

A–19

(A) Solve by substituting the number value for F given in the question and then completing the arithmetic operations:

$C = 5/9(F - 32)$.
$C = 5/9(68 - 32)$.
$C = 5/9(36)$.
$C = 180/9$.
$C = 20$ (choice A).

Celsius/Fahrenheit conversion questions are common, so be sure to increase your comfort level in doing these types of problems.

A–20

(B) First, calculate the discount: $800 \times .25 = 200$. The discounted price is $600.00. Next, subtract the down payment: $600 - 150 = 450$. Divide that price by 12 to determine the amount of the monthly installments: $450 \div 12 = 37.5$ (choice B). Remember to read the question carefully so that you do not miss any steps and also so that you provide the correct answer. Choice A ($50.00) would be correct if no down payment had been made and 12 monthly installments were to be paid on the discounted price of $600.00.

QUESTIONS

Q–21

A blueprint is 30″ wide × 48″ long. If the blueprint is enlarged so that its length measures 80″, how many inches wide will it be?

(A) 50

(B) 60

(C) 48

(D) 42

Your Answer _____

_____

Q–22

At the PX, 5 pounds of hard candies sells for $2.50. How much will an 8-ounce bag cost?

(A) $1.25

(B) $0.50

(C) $0.25

(D) $4.00

Your Answer _____

_____

ANSWERS

A-21

(A) The blueprint and its enlargement will be similar, so the lengths and widths will be in proportion:

$$\frac{\text{length of original}}{\text{length of enlargement}} = \frac{\text{width of original}}{\text{width of enlargement}}$$

Substitute the numbers into the proportion, reduce to lowest terms, and then cross-multiply to get the correct answer:

$$\frac{48}{80} = \frac{30}{x}$$

$$\frac{3}{5} = \frac{30}{x}$$

$$3x = 150$$

$$x = 50$$

The correct answer is A.

A-22

(C) First, determine the cost of 1 pound: $2.50 \div 5 = 0.5$. There are 16 ounces in a pound, so half a pound is 8 ounces. Divide the cost of 1 pound (16 ounces) by 2 to determine the cost of the 8-ounce (half-pound) bag: $0.5 \div 2 = 0.25$. The correct answer is C.

QUESTIONS

The sum of two numbers is 95. One number is 15 more than the other. What is the smaller number?

(A) 40

(B) 50

(C) 35

(D) 15

Your Answer _____

Quentin Carpenter earns $12.50 per hour for every 8-hour workday, with time and a half for overtime. If he works 12 hours on any given day, how much will he earn that day?

(A) $100.00

(B) $175.00

(C) $75.00

(D) $125.00

Your Answer _____

ANSWERS

A–23

(A) Set up an equation equal to 95, where x = the smaller number and $x + 15$ = the larger number: $x + (x + 15) = 95$. Solve for x.

Combine like terms:
$$x + (x + 15) = 95$$
$$2x + 15 = 95$$

Subtract 15 from both sides:
$$2x + 15 - 15 = 95 - 15$$
$$2x = 80$$
$$x = 40 \text{ (choice A)}$$

A–24

(B) Calculate one day's pay at the regular rate: $8 \times 12.5 = 100$. Calculate the rate at time and a half: $12.5 \times 1.5 = 18.75$ (or, $12.5 + 6.25 = 18.75$). Multiply the time-and-a-half rate by the number of hours of overtime: $4 \times 18.75 = 75$. Add the two figures together to get the total pay for that day: $100 + 75 = 175$ (choice B). Remember that time and a half means the original number, plus half again as much.

QUESTIONS

Q-25

Admission to a museum costs $8.00 for adults, $6.00 for seniors and students, and half the adult price for children under 12. On a day when no senior or student admissions were collected, if 350 adult-admission fees were paid, and total fees collected for that day equaled $3,200.00, how many children's admissions were paid?

(A) 100

(B) 400

(C) 700

(D) 800

Your Answer _____

Q-26

Company B has 420 members, and 15% are officers. How many in the company are enlisted personnel?

(A) 85

(B) 63

(C) 405

(D) 357

Your Answer _____

ANSWERS

A–25

(A) Determine the amount collected for adult admissions: $350 \times 8 = 2{,}800$. No senior/student admissions were collected that day, so subtract that amount from the total collection for the day to determine the amount of collected children's admissions: $3{,}200 - 2{,}800 = 400$. Children's admission is $4.00 (half of adult admission [$8.00]), so divide the amount collected by the fee in order to determine the number of children's admissions: $400 \div 4 = 100$ (choice A). Read carefully—this question could not be solved without the figure for seniors/students, unless the instructions specified that no senior/students admissions were collected, which it does.

A–26

(D) If 15% are officers, then 85% are enlisted personnel: $420 \times 0.85 = 357$. Alternatively, calculate 15% of 420, and then subtract: $420 \times 0.15 = 63$; $420 - 63 = 357$. Using either method to solve, the correct answer is D.

QUESTIONS

Q–27

What is the value of $\dfrac{0.03 \times 7}{0.001}$?

(A) 0.210

(B) 210

(C) 21

(D) 0.021

Your Answer _____

_____

Q–28

When the turnpike lifted the toll, traffic increased from 1,500 cars per day to 2,700. What was the percentage of the increase in traffic volume?

(A) 60%

(B) 35%

(C) 80%

(D) 75%

Your Answer _____

_____

ANSWERS

A–27

(B) The first step is to multiply out the numerator:

$$\frac{0.03 \times 7}{0.001} = \frac{0.21}{0.001}$$

Next, clear the decimal in the divider by moving the decimal point three places to the right in both the numerator and the denominator:

$$\frac{0.21}{0.001} = \frac{210}{1} = 210 \text{ (choice B)}$$

Always double-check your work with decimals, and never assume that decimals in the question must mean decimals in the answer.

A–28

(C) The amount of increase is 1,200 (2,700 − 1,500). Divide the amount of increase by the original number: 1,200 ÷ 1,500 = 0.80. Or, set as a fraction and reduce to lowest terms:

$$\frac{1,200}{1,500} = \frac{4}{5}.$$

Whether in decimal or fractional form, this equals 80% (choice C).

QUESTIONS

Q–29

Christina's new cellphone provider charges $0.75 per text for the first 10 words and $0.05 for every additional word. How many words can she text for $3.00?

(A) 45

(B) 35

(C) 55

(D) 225

Your Answer _____

_____

Q–30

Discontinued laptop computers are being sold wholesale for $160.00 each at a 25% discount. An odd-lots merchandiser resells these laptops at a 20% markup above the original wholesale price. What is the profit on each laptop?

(A) $72.00

(B) $32.00

(C) $40.00

(D) $60.00

Your Answer _____

ANSWERS

A-29

(C) The first 10 words cost $0.75, so subtract that amount from the total amount sought: $3.00 - 0.75 = 2.25$. Divide that amount by the cost per each additional word ($0.05): $2.25 \div 0.05 = 45$. The total number of words that can be sent for $3.00 is 55 (10 [for $0.75] + 45 [for $2.25])— choice C. Remember to clear the decimals when dividing, and don't be tricked by forgetting the 10 words included in the basic texting fee.

A-30

(A) Find the discontinued price the merchandiser paid: $160 \times .25 = 40$; $160 - 40 = 120$. Next, find the price the merchandiser will sell the laptop for (20% markup on $160.00): $160 \times 0.20 = 32$; $160 + 32 = 192$. Finally, determine the profit: 192 (selling price) $- 120$ (cost to merchandiser) $= 72$ (choice A). This is a multi-step problem, so be sure to figure out each part of the question and double-check the answer the question instructs you to find before you select your answer choice.

QUESTIONS

Q–31

Col. Roger Blake is retiring from the Air Force, and the company cook is baking a cake in the shape of a B-52 bomber to commemorate the occasion. The cook is using the same recipe his mother used to bake his childhood birthday cakes, plus all the enlisted men's donations of candy bars for the chocolate. The recipe calls for 4½ cups of flour and 3/4 cups of sugar, which the cook will have to quadruple in order to have enough servings. How much sugar will he now need?

(A) 4 cups

(B) 3 cups

(C) 17 cups

(D) 7¼ cups

Your Answer _____

Q–32

Cpl. Jimenez was just promoted to sergeant. Computed hourly, he was earning $10.50, and he received a 6% raise. What is his new hourly rate of pay?

(A) $10.56

(B) $11.13

(C) $16.80

(D) $16.50

Your Answer _____

ANSWERS

A–31

(B)   In spite of all the extra information, all you need to do to solve this problem is multiply 3/4 by 4 (quadruple). Convert to decimal form: $0.75 \times 4 = 3.0$ (choice B). When you come upon a wordy question, beware—but do not allow the unnecessary information to confuse you.

A–32

First, determine the dollar amount that the 6% raise is equal to: $10.50 \times 0.06 = 0.63$. Next, add the amount of the increase to the current hourly salary: $10.50 + 0.63 = 11.13$. Cpl. Jimenez's new hourly rate of pay is $11.13 (choice B). When converting percentages to decimals, always move the decimal point two places to the left: 6.00% becomes 0.06 (adding the decimal in the percent before moving it to the left can help, especially during the actual test).

QUESTIONS

Q–33

In the city of Danford, houses are assessed at 80% of the purchase price. If a home is purchased for $90,000.00 and property taxes are $5.60 per $100.00 of assessed valuation, how much property tax must be paid by the new owners?

(A) $720.00

(B) $4,032.00

(C) $5,040.00

(D) $7,200.00

Your Answer _____

Q–34

A special unit of the Army Corps of Engineers has been formed. In this unit, 75 members have advanced degrees, and 225 have bachelor's degrees. What percentage of the unit have advanced degrees?

(A) 15%

(B) 20%

(C) 30%

(D) 25%

Your Answer _____

ANSWERS

A–33

(B) First, find the assessed value: $90{,}000 \times 0.80 = 72{,}000$. Next, find the number of hundreds in the assessed value: $72{,}000 \div 100 = 720$. Multiply by the tax rate: $720 \times 5.60 = 4{,}032$ (choice B). Again, pay close attention—multi-step problem.

A–34

(D) Calculate the total number of members in the unit: $75 + 225 = 300$. Divide the number with advanced degrees by the total number of members in the unit: $75 \div 300 = 0.25$ (Or, 75/300 reduced to simplest terms = 1/4). Multiply by 100 to represent as a percent: $0.25 \times 100 = 25\%$ (choice D). Read carefully—you have to calculate the total number of members before you can determine the percentage.

QUESTIONS

Q–35

A map measuring 60″ wide × 72″ long must be reduced
and copied to hand out to noncoms leading maneuvers.
If the map is reduced so that its width measures 12″, how
many inches long will it be?

(A) 24

(B) 36

(C) 14.4

(D) 18.2

Your Answer _____

_____

Q–36

Pfc. Walker has patrol duty tonight. He walks the equivalent
of 10 city blocks for every circuit of the camp perimeter.
If he walks at a pace of 5 city blocks every 20 minutes,
how long will it take him to complete a circuit of the
camp perimeter (assuming he is not interrupted by enemy
intruders!)?

(A) 20 minutes

(B) 60 minutes

(C) 50 minutes

(D) 40 minutes

Your Answer _____

_____

ANSWERS

A–35

(C) The map and its reduction will be similar, so the lengths and widths will be in proportion:

$$\frac{\text{width of reduction}}{\text{width of original}} = \frac{\text{length of reduction}}{\text{length of original}}$$

Substitute the numbers into the proportion, reduce to lowest terms, and then cross-multiply to get the correct answer:

$$\frac{12}{60} = \frac{x}{72}$$

$$\frac{1}{5} = \frac{x}{72}$$

$$5x = 72$$

$$x = 14.4 \text{ (choice C)}$$

A–36

(D) Determine how long it takes Pfc. Walker to walk 1 city block by dividing 20 minutes by 5 city blocks: $20 \div 5 = 4$. Multiply that by 10, the number of city blocks equivalent to a circuit of the camp perimeter: $4 \times 10 = 40$. It will take Pfc. Walker 40 minutes to complete a circuit of the camp perimeter (choice D).

QUESTIONS

Q–37

A student scores 78, 87, 80, 84, 91, and 95 on his trigonometry exams during his first semester. Because he has been coming for extra help and to boost his grades, the teacher has agreed to drop his lowest exam score. What is his final average for the course?

(A) 87.4

(B) 85.8

(C) 84

(D) 85

Your Answer _____

Q–38

Maj. Burnside, the attending physician in the infirmary, prescribes vitamin B_{12} to Lt. Hanrahan when he complains of fatigue. If the lieutenant has to take 25 milligrams per day for 30 days, and there are 100 50-milligram vitamin tablets in the bottle, how many vitamin tablets will be left after he finishes his prescribed treatment?

(A) 70

(B) 50

(C) 85

(D) 75

Your Answer _____

ANSWERS

A–37

(A) Drop the lowest score (78), and then add the remaining scores: $87 + 80 + 84 + 91 + 95 = 437$. Divide by the total number of scores to determine the student's final average for the course: $437 \div 5 = 87.4$ (choice A). This is a simple arithmetic problem—don't second-guess yourself into thinking there must be something more complicated to a straightforward question. Just read carefully and enjoy the easy ones when they appear!

A–38

(C) Notice that the doctor prescribed a dosage that is half the amount of the dosage in the bottle: 25 milligrams is half of 50 milligrams. That means that the lieutenant will only need to use 15, not 30, of the vitamins in the bottle, because he can cut each one in half. Subtract the number of vitamins he will need to use from the total number of vitamins in the bottle: $100 - 15 = 85$ (choice C). This is a simple problem, but you need to read carefully in order to realize that the prescribed dosage differs from what is in the bottle.

QUESTIONS

Q–39

The scale on a map is 1/2″ to 40 miles. If the actual distance between the city of Quince and the mouth of the Silver Snake River is 800 miles, how far apart does the mapmaker need to place them when he creates the map?

(A) 20″

(B) 10″

(C) 40″

(D) 5″

Your Answer _____

Q–40

Consider the following numbers: 9, 12, 15, 18, 21, 24, 27. Which term(s) can describe 18?

(A) Mean

(B) Median

(C) Mode

(D) Both mean and median

Your Answer _____

ANSWERS

A–39

(B) Let x = the scaled distance for 800 miles. Use the proportion $\dfrac{\frac{1}{2}}{40} = \dfrac{x}{800}$. Then $40x = \left(\dfrac{1}{2}\right)(800) = 400$.

Thus, $x = \dfrac{400}{40} = 10''$.

A–40

(D) Mean and median are types of averages. Like a simple average, mean can be calculated by adding the numbers together and then dividing by the number of numbers (7): $9 + 12 + 15 + 18 + 21 + 24 + 27 = 126 \div 7 = 18$. Median is the central number within a list of numbers; there are as many numbers above and below it in the list. In this case, 18 is both mean and median (choice D). The mode is the most frequently occurring number; in this case, there is no mode because all the numbers are different.

QUESTIONS

Q–41

Enrollment at a computer technology school increased by 4,000 students between 2000 and 2010, one-quarter more than the admissions office anticipated. How many more students had the admissions office forecasted would enroll in 2010?

(A) 4,400

(B) 5,000

(C) 3,000

(D) 3,200

Your Answer _____

_____

Q–42

After an accident, the two cars involved are towed 20 miles to the nearest garage for repairs. If the tow fee is $5.75 per mile, how much did it cost to tow both vehicles?

(A) $11.50

(B) $115.00

(C) $40.00

(D) $230.00

Your Answer _____

_____

ANSWERS

A–41

(D) Set up an equation where x = the original forecast. An additional one-quarter would be 125% of x: $1.25x = 4,000$. Divide both sides of the equation by 1.25: $x = 3,200$ (choice D). To double-check yourself, divide 3,200 by 4 (that is, multiply it by 1/4) and then add that to 3,200: $800 + 3,200 = 4,000$.

A–42

(D) Multiply the number of miles by the fee: $20 \times 5.75 = 115$. Double the fee to determine the cost for towing two vehicles: $115 \times 2 = 230$ (choice D). Remember, reading carefully is as important as arithmetic ability.

QUESTIONS

Q–43

Cpl. Merritt has bought a house now that his tour of duty is up. He wants to stain the wood floors of the living room, which measures 18′ × 14′. The stain costs $1.20 per square yard. How much will it cost to stain the floor of the entire room?

(A) $21.60

(B) $33.60

(C) $16.80

(D) $302.40

Your Answer _____

_____

Q–44

If the temperatures logged are 80° and 60°, what is the mean temperature?

(A) 65°

(B) 70°

(C) 75°

(D) 72°

Your Answer _____

_____

ANSWERS

A–43

(B)   First, multiply the dimensions of the room to determine the square feet: 18 × 14 = 252. Divide by 9 to convert square feet to square yards: 252 ÷ 9 = 28. Multiply by the cost of stain per square yard: 28 × 1.20 = 33.60. It will cost $33.60 to stain the floor of the entire room (choice B). Questions of this type are common, so remember that 1 square yard = 9 square feet (3 feet × 3 feet). If you have the square feet, just divide by 9 to get the square yards.

A–44

(B)   Remember that the mean is a type of average and can be calculated by adding the numbers and then dividing by the number of items: 80 + 60 = 140 ÷ 2 = 70. The mean temperature is 70° (choice B).

QUESTIONS

Q–45

An X-ray technician earns $14.50 per hour for a 40-hour workweek. His overtime pay is 1½ times his regular pay (base salary). One week, he worked 50 hours. How much did he earn for the 50-hour workweek?

(A) $797.50

(B) $870.00

(C) $580.00

(D) $725.00

Your Answer _____

Q–46

Cmdr. Tucci is stationed in Italy and has received a 3-day pass. He has decided to drive from the base to Rome. The posted speed limit is in kilometers, and his speedometer shows that he is traveling at a rate of 90 kilometers per hour. The commander knows that a kilometer is approximately equal to ⅝ of a mile. Approximately how many miles per hour is he traveling?

(A) 144

(B) 135.25

(C) 56.25

(D) 45.75

Your Answer _____

ANSWERS

A–45

(A) First, calculate the regular pay for a workweek: $14.50 \times 40 = 580.00$. Next, calculate the overtime hourly rate: $14.5 \times 1.5 = 21.75$. Next, calculate the overtime paid for a 50-hour week: $21.75 \times 10 = 217.50$. Add the base pay and overtime together: $580.00 + 217.50 = 797.50$. For a 50-hour workweek at $14.50/hour, the X-ray technician was paid $797.50 (choice A). Remember to check multi-step problems carefully to ensure that you select the correct answer choice.

A–46

(C) A kilometer $= 5/8$ of a mile, so multiply the kilometers per hour by 5/8: $90 \times 5/8 = 450/8 = 56.25$. Or, convert the fraction to a decimal, and then multiply by kmh of 90: $5/8 = 0.625 \times 90 = 56.25$. With either method, the commander is traveling at 56.25 miles per hour (choice C). Conversion problems appear frequently, so remember basic conversion formulas, as well as the decimal forms of common fractions.

QUESTIONS

A painting contractor's bid to paint an office building was accepted. He needs 75 gallons of paint and wants to purchase the paint for the least amount of money he can so that the job will be as profitable as possible. Which of the following is the most cost-effective option?

(A) Three 25-gallon buckets at $300.00 each.

(B) Two 30-gallon buckets at $400.00 each.

(C) One 100-gallon bucket for $1,000.00.

(D) Seventy-five 1-gallon buckets for $20.00 each.

Your Answer _____

ANSWERS

A–47

(A) Determine the cost of each option: $3 \times 300 =$ $900.00; $2 \times 400 = $800.00; $1 \times 1{,}000 = $1{,}000.00$; $75 \times 20 = $1{,}500.00$. The cheapest price is $800.00, but two 30-gallon buckets will provide only 60 gallons, and he needs 75; that eliminates choice B. The other choices all offer a sufficient amount of paint (choice C actually offers 25 gallons more than needed), so just determine which is the cheapest price: $900.00 (choice A). Read, read, read—and then just "do the math!"

QUESTIONS

Q–48

Unit headquarters has 45 enlisted personnel and 5 officers. Per army regulations, each enlisted man's work space can equal no more than 40 square feet. The CO also received notification that 5 more enlisted personnel will be arriving in a week. Currently, the enlisted personnel are using the maximum amount of work space, and the officers will not be giving up any of their work space. How much less work space will each enlisted man have?

(A) 3 square feet less

(B) 3.5 square feet less

(C) 2.5 square feet less

(D) 4 square feet less

Your Answer _____

_____

ANSWERS

A-48

(D) The maximum amount of space is already allotted to each enlisted man, and the officers are keeping their existing space, so calculate the total square footage of the enlisted area by multiplying the square footage for each work space by the current number of enlisted personnel: $40 \times 45 = 1,800$ square feet. Divide that square footage by the new number of enlisted personnel ($45 + 5 = 50$): $1,800/50 = 36$ square feet. Subtract that from the current individual work space square footage: $40 - 36 = 4$. Once the new personnel arrive, each enlisted man will have 4 square feet less space (choice D).

QUESTIONS

Q–49

Two trains left the same station at the same time; one headed west for Denver, and the other headed east for Louisville. The train headed for Denver traveled at 65 miles per hour and the train headed for Louisville traveled at 80 miles per hour. How many miles apart were the trains after 4 hours?

(A) 580

(B) 320

(C) 260

(D) 440

Your Answer _____

_____

Q–50

Mrs. Angstrom has a coupon for 15% off on one salmon steak at her local grocery store, Shop 'n' Save. The salmon steaks cost $7.00 each and she buys 3 of them. How much will the 3 salmon steaks cost if she uses the coupon?

(A) $21.00

(B) $17.85

(C) $19.95

(D) $18.90

Your Answer _____

_____

ANSWERS

A–49

(A) Calculate the distance traveled in 4 hours by the train headed for Denver (miles per hour × number of hours): = 65 × 4 = 260. Do the same for the train headed for Louisville: 80 × 4 = 320. Add the distance figures together: 260 + 320 = 580. After 4 hours, the trains were 580 miles apart. Or, add the rates of speed together and then multiply by the number of hours traveled: 65 + 80 = 145 × 4 = 580. With either method, the correct answer is A.

A–50

(C) First, determine the 15% discount: 7.00 × 0.15 = 1.05. Subtract the discount from the price: 7.00 − 1.05 = 5.95. The other two salmon steaks are full-price: 7.00 × 2 = 14.00. Add together the one discounted salmon steak and the two at regular price: 5.95 + 14.00 = 19.95. The three salmon steaks, with the 15% coupon, will cost $19.95 (choice C). The arithmetic here is simple, but remember to check for what the question is asking. Only one salmon steak is reduced by 15%.

QUESTIONS

Q–51

A Jeep uses gasoline at the rate of 24 miles per gallon. Pfc. Romano did not realize she was low on fuel when she left base. Off base, gasoline costs $3.06 per gallon, and she drives 3 hours at 60 miles per hour to get back to base on time. How much did she have to pay for the gas for her trip back to base?

(A) $21.00

(B) $22.95

(C) $29.09

(D) $24.00

Your Answer _____

_____

Q–52

A hexahedral die is rolled three times. What is the probability of NOT rolling a 4 any of the three times?

(A) 4/36

(B) 36/256

(C) 64/216

(D) 125/216

Your Answer _____

_____

ANSWERS

A–51

(B) First, determine the number of miles traveled by multiplying rate of speed by time traveled: $3 \times 60 = 180$. Next, determine the amount of gas used by dividing the miles traveled by the miles per gallon: $180 \div 24 = 7.5$. Multiply that by the price per gallon: $7.5 \times 3.06 = 22.95$. The trip cost $22.95 (choice B). Note that you do not need to know how many gallons of gasoline the tank holds. Questions of this type will often include an answer choice that says you cannot determine the answer without knowing how many gallons of gas the tank holds. Don't be fooled!

A–52

(D) The probability of rolling a 4 is 1 out of 6 (1/6), so the probability of NOT rolling a 4 is $1 - 1/6$, or 5/6. The probability of not rolling a 4 three times is $5/6 \times 5/6 \times 5/6 = 125/216$ (choice D). Do not be confused by the term "hexahedral," which means six-sided figure—a die, like all cubes, is hexahedral. This is a simple probability question. All you need to do is read carefully to notice that the question asks for the probability of NOT rolling a 4 any of the three times.

QUESTIONS

Q–53

If a company pays the following hourly rates: $3.00, $4.00, $5.00, $8.00, and $10.00, what is the median rate?

(A) $6.00

(B) $5.00

(C) $5.50

(D) $6.50

Your Answer _____

Q–54

A half-pint of milk is equivalent to what part of a gallon?

(A) 1/2

(B) 3/4

(C) 1/16

(D) 1/8

Your Answer _____

ANSWERS

A–53

(B) Median is the central number within a list of numbers; in other words, there are as many numbers above and below it in the list. In this case, $5.00 (choice B). Remember the difference between mean (simple average), median (central number), and mode (most frequently occurring number).

A–54

(C) A gallon equals 8 pints, or 16 half-pints. Therefore, one half-pint = 1/16 of a gallon (choice C). Easy if you remember those conversions!

QUESTIONS

Q–55

A 2½-ton truck with four axles is taxed at a rate of $0.09 per pound. How much must the trucking company pay in taxes for this truck?

(A) $225.00

(B) $180.00

(C) $360.00

(D) $450.00

Your Answer _____

Q–56

Sgt. Munch stops in at the PX to buy some energy bars prior to a 50-mile hike. The cost has increased from $1.25 to $1.40 per bar. What is the percent increase?

(A) 15%

(B) 12%

(C) 10%

(D) 8%

Your Answer _____

ANSWERS

A–55

(D) Convert the tonnage to pounds and multiply by the per-pound tax rate to determine the taxes due: 5,000 × 0.09 = 450. The trucking company must pay $450.00 in taxes (choice D). Remember that 1 ton is equal to 2,000 pounds, so 2½ tons is equal to 5,000 pounds. Note that the number of axles is unnecessary information.

A–56

(B) Determine the difference in cost by subtracting the old price from the new price: 1.40 − 1.25 = 0.15. Divide the difference in price by the old price and then multiply by 100 to find the percent increase: 0.15 ÷ 1.25 = 0.12 × 100 = 12% (choice B). Nothing to fool you on this one!

QUESTIONS

Q–57

Sally has a shoebox filled with loose change: 15 half-dollars, 25 quarters, 45 dimes, 30 nickels, and 95 pennies. She wants to bring the coins to the bank and receive bills in exchange once she has $25.00 worth of coins. How much more money does she need to save?

(A) $6.20

(B) $3.80

(C) $4.30

(D) $5.60

Your Answer _____

Q–58

Bruce has been a menswear salesman for 35 years. Currently, he earns $150.00/week plus a 10% commission on any sales. In a week where he has $750.00 in sales, what is the ratio of his commission to his salary?

(A) 1/2

(B) 1/3

(C) 2/1

(D) 3/1

Your Answer _____

ANSWERS

A–57

(C) Determine the value in dollars of all the loose change:
15 half-dollars (15 × 0.50 = 7.50) + 25 quarters (25 ×
0.25 = 6.25) + 45 dimes (45 × 10 = 4.50) + 30 nickels
(30 × 0.05 = 1.50) + 95 pennies (95 × 0.01 = 0.95) =
20.70. Subtract that amount from the total she wants to have
before exchanging the coins for bills: 25.00 − 20.70 =
4.30. Sally needs to save $4.30 more in coins (choice C).

A–58

(A) First, calculate his commission for the week:
750.00 × 0.10 = 75.00. The ratio of his commission to
his salary is 75/150, or 1/2 (choice A). Do not be distracted
by the 35-year tenure, which will not help you solve the
problem.

QUESTIONS

Q–59

Reveille is at 0515 hours. The bugler, Cpl. Woogie, usually rises at 0435 hours in order to be ready in time, but this morning he overslept and did not awaken until 0447 hours. How much less time will he have to get ready?

(A) 12 minutes

(B) 22 minutes

(C) 28 minutes

(D) 40 minutes

Your Answer _____

_____

Q–60

Larry works for 5 hours and is paid $42.00. His coworker, Max, works for 4 hours and is paid $29.00. How much more per hour does Larry earn than Max?

(A) $1.30

(B) $1.15

(C) $2.50

(D) $2.15

Your Answer _____

_____

ANSWERS

A–59

(A) From 0435 to 0515 is 40 minutes. From 0447 to 0515 is 28 minutes. Calculate the difference: $40 - 28 = 12$. Cpl. Woogie will have 12 fewer minutes to get ready this morning (choice A). You could also calculate the amount of time he overslept ($0447 - 0435 = 0012$).

A–60

(B) Calculate Larry's hourly rate of pay: $42.00 \div 5 = 8.40$. Calculate Max's hourly rate of pay: $29.00 \div 4 = 7.25$. Subtract Max's hourly rate of pay from Larry's: $8.40 - 7.25 = 1.15$. Larry earns \$1.15 more per hour than Max does (choice B). No tricks in this question!

QUESTIONS

Q–61

Which is the closest approximation of a quart in terms of liters?

(A) 1 liter

(B) 0.75 liter

(C) 0.5 liter

(D) 1.5 liters

Your Answer _____

Q–62

A nonprofit organization has to downsize, so it offers an early retirement incentive to the 55-year-old receptionist, Hortense. Because she is too young to cash out a tax-deferred investment without incurring a penalty, Hortense opts to roll over the 403(b) qualified plan to a new IRA. The total amount of the rollover is $10,000.00. If she doesn't deposit or withdraw any monies, and the IRA earns 5½% interest annually, how much money will be in her account in a year?

(A) $550.00

(B) $10,000.00

(C) $10,550.00

(D) $10,500.00

Your Answer _____

ANSWERS

A–61

(A) A liter equals 33.8 fluid ounces, or 1 quart (32 fluid ounces) plus 1.8 fluid ounces. The closest approximation of a quart in terms of liters is 1 liter (choice A).

A–62

(C) You do not need to know about tax-deferred investments or tax regulations. This is a simple arithmetic problem. First, determine the amount of interest earned by multiplying the amount of the investment by the interest rate (convert the percentage to a decimal by moving the decimal point two places to the left): $10,000 \times 0.055 = 550$. Add that amount to the principal investment ($10,000.00): $550 + 10,000 = 10,550$. At the end of a year, Hortense will have $10,550.00 in her IRA (choice C).

QUESTIONS

Q–63

Determine the square footage of linoleum needed to cover a 13′ × 13′ room.

(A) 26 square feet

(B) 52 square feet

(C) 169 square feet

(D) 130 square feet

Your Answer _____

Q–64

Find the mode: 37, 52, 73, 109, 37, 91, 109, 73, 37, 55, 106.

(A) 37

(B) 73

(C) 109

(D) 55

Your Answer _____

ANSWERS

A–63

(C) Determine square footage by calculating the area (that is, multiplying length × width): 13 × 13 = 169 (choice C). Do not confuse area (length × width) with perimeter (sum of all sides). Square footage is not necessarily a square number, but because the lengths of the sides are equal in this case, the area is a square number.

A–64

(A) Mode is the most frequently occurring number. In this case, 37 appears three times, so it is the mode (choice A). Consider the other answers: 73 and 109 both appear twice, and 55 only appears once; the answer must be one that is the only one that can stand alone as a true answer, so even if you do not remember the meaning of mode, only one number appears three times: 37. Multiple numbers appear twice and/or once, which rules them all out as choices.

QUESTIONS

Q–65

The CO of a Navy Seal unit orders all members to run 6 miles. The track they are assigned to use is 3/4 of a mile around. How many laps do they each need to run?

(A) 6

(B) 8

(C) 4.5

(D) 9

Your Answer _____

_____

ANSWERS

(B) Convert the fraction to a decimal: $3/4 = 0.75$. Next, divide the total number of miles by one lap: $6 \div 0.75 = 8$ (choice B). Alternatively, multiply by the reciprocal: $6 \times 4/3 = 24/3 = 8$.

QUESTIONS

Q–66

What is the cube root of 125?

(A) 5

(B) 25

(C) 15

(D) 125 has no cube root

Your Answer _____

_____

Q–67

$(y + 9)(y + 7) =$

(A) $y^2 + 63y + 63$

(B) $y^2 + 16y + 16$

(C) $y^2 + 16y + 63$

(D) $y^2 + 63y + 16$

Your Answer _____

_____

ANSWERS

A–66

(A) This is the reverse of asking, "What is 5 cubed?"
$5 \times 5 \times 5 = 125$, so the cube root of 125 is 5 (choice A).
The other answers are incorrect. Think very carefully
before choosing any answer implying that there is no
correct answer listed.

A–67

(C) Multiply the first variable in each set of parentheses:
y ($y \times y = y^2$). Follow this multiplication step for each part
of each set of parentheses: ($y \times 9 = 9y$), ($y \times 7 = 7y$),
($9 \times 7 = 63$). So, $y^2 + 9y + 7y + 63$. Combine like terms
to get the correct answer: $y^2 + 16y + 63$ (choice C). The
other choices, all of which involve misinterpretation of
when to add and when to multiply, are incorrect.

QUESTIONS

Q–68

A triangle with angles measuring 45°, 60°, and 75° would be a(n) _____ triangle.

(A) right

(B) scalene

(C) equilateral

(D) isosceles

Your Answer _____

Q–69

Find the numerical value of $3 + 4xy^2 - 5x^2y$ if $x = 3$ and $y = 4$.

(A) 195

(B) 180

(C) 15

(D) 375

Your Answer _____

ANSWERS

A–68

(B) Remember that all angles in a triangle must total 180°. A scalene triangle is one whose angles all have different measurements, so the correct answer is B. A right triangle must have one angle measuring 90°. The angles of an equilateral triangle all have equal measurements (that is, all are 60°). An isosceles triangle must have two equivalent angles.

A–69

(C) Substitute the values given into the equation $3 + 4xy^2 - 5x^2y$.

$3 + 4\,(3)(4^2) - 5\,(3^2)(4)$
$3 + 4\,(3)(16) - 5\,(9)(4)$
$3 + 4 \times 48 - 5 \times 36$
$3 + 192 - 180$
$195 - 180 = 15$ (choice C).

QUESTIONS

Q–70

In mathematical terms, which of the following pairs of objects is an example of similar figures?

(A) A circle and an oval

(B) A car and a scale model of that car

(C) An octagon and a hexagon

(D) A square and a rectangle

Your Answer _____

Q–71

If the circumference of a circle is divided by the length of its diameter, what is the result?

(A) 22

(B) π

(C) 7

(D) Cannot be determined from the information given

Your Answer _____

ANSWERS

A–70

(B) In mathematical terms, two objects are similar if they are the same shape, regardless of whether they are the same size. Of the choices given, only the car and its scale model are similar (choice B) because none of the other objects have the same shape. When a question specifies a certain terminology, be sure to think carefully about what that means before choosing your answer.

A–71

(B) The formula for circumference of a circle is $C = \pi \times D$ (diameter). $C \div D = \pi$. The correct answer is B. The other choices are incorrect. You do not need to know the actual measurements of the circumference and the diameter in order to answer this question, and you should always beware of answer choices that indicate the question cannot be answered from the information provided. Note that an alternate formula for circumference is $C = \pi \times 2R$ (radius—the radius is half the diameter).

QUESTIONS

Q–72

Use the following formula, $I = \sqrt{\dfrac{P}{R}}$,

to find the value of I when $P = 144$ and $R = 16$.

(A) 12

(B) 4

(C) 3

(D) 0

Your Answer _____

Q–73

Give the next term in the series: $2\frac{1}{4}$, $5\frac{3}{4}$, 8, $11\frac{1}{2}$, $13\frac{3}{4}$, ____.

(A) 18

(B) 15

(C) $16\frac{1}{4}$

(D) $17\frac{1}{4}$

Your Answer _____

ANSWERS

A–72

(C) Substitute the values given into the equation:

$$I = \sqrt{\dfrac{P}{R}}$$

$$I = \sqrt{\dfrac{144}{16}}$$

$$I = \sqrt{9}$$

$I = 3$ (choice C).

Remember that the square root of a number is the number which, when multiplied by itself equals that number. $3 \times 3 = 9$, so the square root of 9 is 3.

A–73

(D) Establish the relationship between each term:

$2\frac{1}{4}$, $5\frac{3}{4}$ $(+3\frac{1}{2})$
$5\frac{3}{4}$, 8 $(+2\frac{1}{4})$
8, $11\frac{1}{2}$ $(+3\frac{1}{2})$
$11\frac{1}{2}$, $13\frac{3}{4}$ $(+2 \frac{1}{4})$

Therefore, the next relationship must be $+3\frac{1}{2}$: $13\frac{3}{4} + 3\frac{1}{2} = 17\frac{1}{4}$ (choice D). Note that this might be simpler if you convert the fractions to decimals: 1/4 = 0.25; 1/2 = 0.50; 3/4 = 0.75.

QUESTIONS

Q–74

A solid figure with four faces is called a _____.

(A) square

(B) cube

(C) hexahedron

(D) tetrahedron

Your Answer _____

_____

Q–75

4 and 16 are the fourth root and the square root, respectively, of what number?

(A) 64

(B) 144

(C) 96

(D) 256

Your Answer _____

_____

ANSWERS

A–74

(D) A solid figure with 4 faces is called a tetrahedron (choice D). A hexahedron is a solid figure with 6 faces; a cube is an example of a hexahedron. A square is not a solid figure.

A–75

(D) The fourth root is the reverse of x^4 and the square root is the reverse of x^2. In other words, what number $= 4 \times 4 \times 4 \times 4$ and also $= 16 \times 16$? The answer is 256 (choice D). Notice that 4 is the square root of 16.

QUESTIONS

Q–76

A line connecting points on a curve is called a(n)
_____.

(A) ellipse

(B) chord

(C) arc

(D) diameter

Your Answer _____

Q–77

If $xy = 15$ and $x^2 + y^2 = 50$, solve for a in the equation $a = (x + y)^2$.

(A) 225

(B) 100

(C) 30

(D) 80

Your Answer _____

ANSWERS

A–76

(B) Any line connecting points on a curve is called a chord. The diameter is the line that connects two points on a round figure, but it must divide that figure in half. An arc is any portion of the circumference of a round figure (that is, a curve). An ellipse is a round shape, but it is not a perfect circle. The correct answer is B.

A–77

(D) You need to expand the equation in order to solve it: $a = x^2 + y^2 + 2xy$. You already know that $x^2 + y^2 = 50$ and $xy = 15$. Substitute these known values into the equation: $a = 50 + 2(15)$. Solving for a results in $a = 80$ (choice D). No shortcuts here; just set up the equation, substitute, and then solve.

QUESTIONS

Q–78

Angela inherited her grandfather's pizzeria. Her cousin just texted to say he'll be coming over in 10 minutes, and he's starving! Feeling sorry for him, she cuts a freshly baked pie in half, and then cuts a line with her pizza cutter from the center to the edge, which creates a 65° angle, so she can give him a nice big slice! What is the supplement of the 65° angle?

(A) 145°

(B) 115°

(C) 125°

(D) 110°

Your Answer _____

Q–79

Cpl. Wayne can do 1/4 of a job by herself in one day, and her assistant, Pfc. Grayson, can do 1/6 of the job by himself in one day. What portion of the job can they do if they work together for one day?

(A) 1/5

(B) 1/3

(C) 3/8

(D) 5/12

Your Answer _____

ANSWERS

A–78

(B) It's nice that Angela inherited her grandfather's pizzeria and that she's carrying on the family tradition. She sure is generous to give her cousin a great big slice, and she probably won't charge him for it, either. But this question is really just about supplementary angles. If she cut a piece that created a 65° angle, all you have to do is subtract that from 180° to get the answer: $180 - 65 = 115$ (choice B). Remember to memorize those geometry rules!

A–79

(D) Add the portions of work to find out what they can accomplish working together: 1/4 + 1/6. Fractions must have a common denominator before they can be added. The least common denominator (smallest number that both can divide into evenly) for 4 and 6 is 12, so change 1/4 and 1/6 to equivalent fractions with 12 as the denominator, and then add them together: $3/12 + 2/12 = 5/12$ (choice D).

QUESTIONS

Q–80

The perimeter of a square is 14′4″. What is the length of one side of the square?

(A) 4′1″

(B) 3′1″

(C) 7′2″

(D) 3′7″

Your Answer _____

_____

Q–81

Solve for y: $2y + 6 = 15 - y$.

(A) 9

(B) 2

(C) 5

(D) 3

Your Answer _____

_____

ANSWERS

A–80

(D) The perimeter of a square is the sum of the lengths of all four sides, and all sides of a square are of equal length. The perimeter equals 14′4″. Change feet to inches (1′ = 12″), and then divide by 4 (number of sides): 14′ (168″) + 4″ = 172″. 172 ÷ 4 = 43. Convert back to feet and inches, combined, to get the correct answer: 3′7″ (choice D).

A–81

(D) Isolate all terms containing y on one side of the equation and all terms not containing y on the other side. That means adding y to both sides and subtracting 6 from both sides:

$$2y + y + 6 - 6 = 15 - 6 - y + y$$
$$3y = 9$$

Divide by 3 to solve for y: $y = 3$ (choice D). Remember to change the sign of any term when moving it from one side of the equation to the other.

QUESTIONS

Q–82

The symbol $\sqrt[3]{}$ represents _____.

(A) a cube root

(B) a square root

(C) a factorial

(D) a trinomial

Your Answer _____

_____

Q–83

Which of the following is a prime number?

(A) 9

(B) 13

(C) 15

(D) 21

Your Answer _____

_____

ANSWERS

A–82

(A) $\sqrt[3]{}$ is the symbol for cube root (choice A). This is an instance where you simply have to be able to identify the symbol. Do not be confused by square root as a choice; it would be the radical sign without a number.

A–83

(B) A prime number is any number that is divisible only by itself and 1 (choice B). Each of the other numbers is divisible by other numbers as well by itself and 1 (9 is divisible by 3; 15 is divisible by 3 and 5; 21 is divisible by 3 and 7).

QUESTIONS

Q–84

If the larger angle of a pair of complementary angles = 65°, what is the measure of the smaller angle in the pair?

(A) 15°

(B) 25°

(C) 30°

(D) 10°

Your Answer _____

Q–85

6 factorial = _____.

(A) 6 and 1

(B) 2 and 3

(C) 1, 2, 3, 6

(D) 6 × 5 × 4 × 3 × 2 × 1

Your Answer _____

ANSWERS

A–84

(B) Complementary angles must equal 90°, so subtract the measure of the larger angle (65°) to determine the measure of the smaller angle in the pair: 90 − 65 = 25. The smaller of the pair of complementary angles measures 25° (choice B).

A–85

(D) 6 factorial is represented as 6 × 5 × 4 × 3 × 2 × 1 (choice D). The symbol for 6 factorial is 6!. Do not confuse *factorial* with *factor,* which is a divisor of a whole number other than that number and 1 (that is, 2 and 3 are factors of 6).

QUESTIONS

Q–86

Which of the following is NOT a quadratic equation?

(A) $y^2 + y - 5 = 0$

(B) $4a^2 = 7a - 3$

(C) $7b^2 + 8yz - 3$

(D) $256 = x^2$

Your Answer _____

Q–87

Find the value of $-y^4$ if $y = 0.2$.

(A) -0.8

(B) -0.08

(C) -0.16

(D) -0.0016

Your Answer _____

ANSWERS

A–86

(C) A quadratic equation is an equation that has a term with the square of an unknown quantity but that has no term with a higher power of the unknown. Choices A, B, and D are all quadratic equations. Choice C is not an equation; it is a trinomial. The question asks which is NOT a quadratic equation, so the correct answer is C.

A–87

(D) $-y^4 = -(y)(y)(y)(y)$. Substitute 0.2 for y: $-y^4 = -(0.2)(0.2)(0.2)(0.2)$. $-y^4 = -0.0016$ (choice D). Remember when multiplying that the number of decimal places in the product is the total number of decimal places in the numbers being multiplied together.

QUESTIONS

Q-88

A figure with five angles and five sides is called a
_____.

(A) pentagon

(B) quincunx

(C) quinquefoil

(D) pentagram

Your Answer _____

Q-89

M.Sgt. Swift must drive from base 8 miles due west and then 6 miles due south. When he arrives at his destination, how many miles is he from his starting point (the base)?

(A) 6

(B) 8

(C) 14

(D) 10

Your Answer _____

ANSWERS

A–88

(A) A figure with 5 angles and 5 sides is called a pentagon (choice D). A pentagram is more commonly known as a five-pointed star. The other choices are not geometric shapes. Just think of the Pentagon building (headquarters of the U.S. Department of Defense).

A–89

(D) M.Sgt. Swift's path due west forms a right angle with his path due south, so the distance from the starting point is measured on the third side (hypotenuse) of this right triangle, which contains the paths to the west and the south. You need to use the Pythagorean Theorem (in any right triangle, the square of the hypotenuse [c^2] = the square of the other two sides [$a^2 + b^2$]): $c^2 = 8^2 + 6^2$; $c^2 = 64 + 36$; $c^2 = 100$). Therefore, $c = 10$ (10 is the square root of 100; or, $10 \times 10 = 100$). M. Sgt. Swift is 10 miles from his starting point (the base) when he reaches his destination (choice D). Geometry rules again!

QUESTIONS

Q–90

A Jeep tire has a diameter of 20″. How many inches will the tire roll during a single rotation? (Use 3.14 as the value of π.)

(A) 62.8

(B) 125.6

(C) 3.14

(D) 23.14

Your Answer _____

_____

Q–91

From $10y^2 - 6y$ subtract $3y - 4y^2$.

(A) $7y^2 - 2y$

(B) $6y^2 - 3y$

(C) $14y^2 - 9y$

(D) $14y^2 - 3y$

Your Answer _____

_____

ANSWERS

A–90

(A) A single rotation of a wheel is the same as "laying out" its circumference. Use the formula for circumference of a circle: $C = \pi \times D$ (diameter). $C = 3.14 \times 20 = 62.8$ (choice A). Note that sometimes the formula is expressed as $C = 2 \times \pi \times R$ (radius, which is half the diameter).

A–91

(C) **Step 1:** Place the binomial to be subtracted under the binomial it is to be subtracted from:

$10y^2 - 6y$

$- 4y^2 + 3y$

Step 2: Change the signs of the terms in the bottom row, and then combine the similar terms in each column:

$10y^2 - 6y$

$4y^2 - 3y$

$14y^2 - 9y$

The correct answer is C. When setting up the subtraction, make sure to line up similar terms in each column. Also, make sure to change the signs after you move the terms, as shown in step 2.

QUESTIONS

Q–92

The symbol ∉ means _____.

(A) element of

(B) not an element of

(C) intersection of

(D) sum of

Your Answer _____

Q–93

If $a = 2$, what is the value of $|a - 9|$?

(A) −11

(B) 7

(C) −7

(D) 11

Your Answer _____

ANSWERS

A–92

(B) In set theory, the symbol ∉ means "not an element of" (choice B). The other choices listed have the following symbols: ∈, ∩, Σ —for element of, intersection of, and sum of (or summation), respectively.

A–93

(B) Substitute the value given for *a*. So, $|a - 9|$ becomes $|2 - 9|$, or $|-7|$; but $|-7|$ stands for the absolute value of -7, which is 7 (choice B). This question tests knowledge of math operators (absolute value notation $|x|$). It also tests how to use the math operator: knowing that absolute value means the positive value of a number regardless of its sign— in other words, the absolute value of a number is the same whether it is positive or negative, so $|-7|$ and $|7|$ are 7.

QUESTIONS

Q–94

An octagon has 8 sides and 8 angles. Given that information, which best describes an octahedron?

(A) It is the same as an octagon.

(B) It is an eight-pointed star.

(C) It is a three-dimensional octagon.

(D) It is a solid figure with 8 faces.

Your Answer _____

Q–95

Give the product of $4a^3b$ and $(6a^2b - 3)$.

(A) $24a^6b^2 - 12$

(B) $24a^6b^2 - 12\,a^6b$

(C) $24a^5b^2 - 12\,a^3b$

(D) $24a^6b^2 - 3$

Your Answer _____

ANSWERS

A–94

(D) An octahedron is a solid figure with 8 faces (choice D). Although, as a solid figure, it has three dimensions, it is not necessarily a three-dimensional octagon.

A–95

(C) Multiply $4a^3b$ by $6a^2b$ and also multiply $4a^3b$ by -3:

Step 1

$4a^3b \times 6a^2b$

$4 \times 6 = 24$ (multiply the numerical factors)

$a^3 \times a^2 = a^5$ and $b \times b = b^2$ (multiply the powers of like letters, and remember to add the exponents)

$24a^5b^2$

Step 2

$4a^3b \times -3$

$-12\,a^3b$

Therefore, the product of $4a^3b$ and $(6a^2b - 3)$ is $24a^5b^2 - 12\,a^3b$ (choice C). In multiplication problems like these, remember that the exponents are added together, not multiplied (choice B is a trick). Also, when a letter appears without an exponent it means "to the first power" (b is the same as b^1).

QUESTIONS

Q–96

Give the number of feet in a length that equals y yards and i inches.

(A) $\dfrac{12i + y}{3}$

(B) $\dfrac{36y + i}{12}$

(C) $12i + 3y$

(D) $36i + y$

Your Answer _____

_____

Q–97

A line is drawn perpendicular to the base of an equilateral triangle from one of the triangle's vertices. What is the measure of the angle made by the perpendicular line and the other side of the triangle that contains this vertex?

(A) 60°

(B) 90°

(C) 45°

(D) 30°

Your Answer _____

_____

ANSWERS

A-96

(B) First, convert all units to inches. There are 36″ in a yard, so in *y* yards there are *y* times as many, or 36*y*; the total length of *y* yards and *i* inches, expressed in inches, is 36*y* + *i* inches. There are 12″ in a foot, so in order to find the number of feet in 36*y* + *i* inches, divide 36*y* + *i* by 12. The answer must be an expression that reflects that statement. The only one that does is choice B, which is the correct answer. The other answers are written to be deliberately confusing; the only way to get the correct answer here is to follow the process outlined above.

A-97

(D) The perpendicular line will create a right angle (90°) with the base. An equilateral triangle has 3 equal sides and 3 equal angles; because the sum of the 3 angles in a triangle must always equal 180°, each angle in an equilateral triangle must equal 60° (180° ÷ 3). Therefore, you must subtract a 60° angle from the 90° in order to get the answer sought: 90 − 60 = 30. The angle formed by the perpendicular line and the other side of the triangle is 30° (choice D).

QUESTIONS

Q–98

Solve the following inequality: $x - 8 \leq 7$.

(A) $x \leq 15$

(B) $x \leq 1$

(C) $x < 15$

(D) $x < 1$

Your Answer _____

Q–99

The null set can be represented as

(A) ó.

(B) ô.

(C) $\varnothing$.

(D) θ.

Your Answer _____

ANSWERS

A-98

(A) The statement $x - 8 \leq 7$ means that the x minus 8 is less than or equal to 7. To solve, isolate x on one side by adding 8 to both sides:

$x - 8 + 8 \leq 7 + 8$

$x \leq 15$ (choice A)

To double check, substitute any number less than or equal to 15 and see if it works: $13 - 8 \leq 7$ (true: $13 - 8 = 5$, which is less than 7). Solving inequalities can be intimidating, but if you always substitute a number into the solution to see if it works, you can easily see if you solved correctly.

A-99

(C) The symbol for the null set is $\varnothing$. Choices A and B are letters from foreign alphabets. Choice D, the lowercase theta (Greek alphabet), is often confused with the null symbol; although it is used in advanced math and science, it has nothing to do with the null set. The correct answer is C.

QUESTIONS

Q–100

Find the numerical value of $2 + 6ab^2 - 3a^2b$ if $a = 5$ and $b = 3$.

(A) 47

(B) 50

(C) 90

(D) 95

Your Answer _____

Q–101

A dodecagon is a figure with

(A) 13 sides and 13 angles.

(B) 12 sides and 12 angles.

(C) 14 sides and 14 angles.

(D) 11 sides and 11 angles.

Your Answer _____

ANSWERS

A–100

(A) Substitute the values given into the equation $2 + 6ab^2 - 3a^2b$.

$2 + 6\,(5)(3^2) - 3\,(5^2)(3)$
$2 + (30)(9) - 3\,(25)(3)$
$2 + 270 - 3 \times 75$
$272 - 225$
$272 - 225 = 47$ (choice A).

A–101

(B) A dodecagon is a figure with 12 sides and 12 angles (choice B). This question tests rote memorization of geometric shapes. Unless you can count in Greek, you have to remember that *dodeca* = 12 (*deca* = 10, *hendeca* = 11, and so forth). Generally, 12 is the highest number that the test uses.

QUESTIONS

Q–102

Which of the following everyday items is an example of a hexagonal prism?

(A)   An unsharpened pencil

(B)   A ball-peen hammer

(C)   A salad fork

(D)   A toothbrush

Your Answer _____

_____

Q–103

If $x - 6 = 3$, then x is equal to

(A)   12.

(B)   6.

(C)   9.

(D)   13.

Your Answer _____

_____

ANSWERS

A–102

(A) A prism is a solid object whose bases (ends) have the same size or shape and are parallel to each other; the bases of a hexagonal prism are—you guessed it—hexagons (polygons with 6 sides and 6 angles). An unsharpened pencil, if it is 6-sided, is a hexagonal prism (choice A). Note that the sharpened end of the pencil becomes a cone. None of the other examples are hexagonal prisms.

A–103

(C) The math in this equation is simple enough that you can get the right answer without following the steps to solve the equation. However, you should be comfortable doing the solving steps, just in case. This equation is really asking, "What number minus 6 equals 3?" The answer is 9 (choice C). To reach this answer by following actual solving steps, isolate x by adding 6 to both sides of the equation:

$x - 6 + 6 = 3 + 6$
$x = 9$

If you do take the shortcut, plug the number into the equation to make sure you are right before selecting your answer:

$x - 6 = 3$
$9 - 6 = 3$

QUESTIONS

Q–104

If $p > q$ and $q > r$, which of these statements is true?

(A) $p > r$

(B) $p < r$

(C) $q = r$

(D) $q + r = p + q$

Your Answer _____

Q–105

Which symbol means *intersection*?

(A) $\perp$

(B) $\cap$

(C) $\dagger$

(D) $\vdash$

Your Answer _____

ANSWERS

A–104

(A) If $p > q$ and $q > r$, then $p > r$ (choice A). This question is a simple test of your knowledge of the Transitive Property of Inequality: $a > b$ and $b > c$, then $a > c$; all that's changed here are the letters. None of the other choices could possibly be true because of what this property states. Memorize those rules!

A–105

(B) In set theory, intersection is represented by the symbol $\cap$ (choice B). Note that the question does not specify set theory, so you need to identify the symbol by sight. The other choices may "look like" intersections, but that is not what they represent. Choice A is the geometric symbol for perpendicular; choices C and D are not mathematical symbols.

QUESTIONS

Q–106

Which of the following is an example of a pyramid with a triangular base?

(A)   The Empire State Building

(B)   The Great Pyramid of Giza

(C)   The Washington Monument

(D)   None of the above

Your Answer _____

_____

Q–107

Which of the following could be used as a simple definition for a postulate?

(A)   A solid figure with 4 or more sides.

(B)   A statement that solves a quadratic equation.

(C)   An assumption that is used as basis for how math works.

(D)   A statement that proves a geometric principle.

Your Answer _____

_____

ANSWERS

A–106

(D) This is a trick question—none of the structures listed is a pyramid with a triangular base, including the Great Pyramid of Giza, which is a pyramid with a square base. The correct answer is D. Although you should be careful before choosing "none of the above" as your answer, sometimes it is correct. Always read carefully and be alert to questions that seem too easy, as this would be if the correct answer choice to a question about pyramids contained the word *pyramid*.

A–107

(C) The only choice listed that could be used as a simple definition for a postulate is "an assumption that is used as a basis for how math works" (choice C). The key here is knowing that postulates are *assumptions*. None of the other answers is correct.

QUESTIONS

Q–108

In a regular heptagon, all the angles are equal and one of them is $128\frac{4}{7}^{\circ}$. What is the sum of all the angles in the regular heptagon?

(A) 660°

(B) 900°

(C) 990°

(D) 360°

Your Answer _____

Q–109

S.Sgt. Henderson has finished 5 reports for his CO, Maj. Briggs. These 5 reports are 10% of the amount of reports that are due. What is the number of total reports due?

(A) 100

(B) 25

(C) 75

(D) 50

Your Answer _____

ANSWERS

A–108

(B) A heptagon is a polygon with 7 sides and 7 angles. The sum of 7 equal angles is 7 times the size of one angle:

$7 \times 128\frac{4}{7} = 7 \times \frac{900}{7} = 900$ (choice B). Here again

is a question that requires memorization of geometric principles and terms. A and C would be the correct answer for a regular hexagon and nonagon, respectively, with equal angles of 110°; 360° is the total number of degrees in a circle.

A–109

(D) The total number of reports due = 100%, and we know that S.Sgt. Henderson has finished 10% of the total. Divide 100 by 10, and then multiply by the actual number of completed reports (5) in order to determine the total number of reports due: $100 \div 10 = 10 \times 5 = 50$. The total number of reports due is 50 (choice D).

QUESTIONS

Q–110

$(y^4)^2 =$

(A) y^8.

(B) y^6.

(C) y^2.

(D) y^{-6}.

Your Answer _____

Q–111

Which of the following is NOT an example of a parallelogram?

(A) Square

(B) Rectangle

(C) Rhombus

(D) Nonagon

Your Answer _____

ANSWERS

A–110

(A) $(y^4)^2 = y^8$. Exponents combined in this way should be multiplied. The correct answer is A. The only way to arrive at the correct answer is to know the rules for how to deal with exponents.

A–111

(D) A nonagon is a figure with 9 angles and 9 sides; it is not a parallelogram. All the other figures are examples of parallelograms, so the correct answer is D.

QUESTIONS

Q–112

What is the reciprocal of 8/5?

(A) 40

(B) 1.6

(C) 5/8

(D) 3

Your Answer _____

Q–113

If one of the two equal angles in an isosceles triangle measures 55°, how much does the angle opposite the unequal side measure?

(A) 50°

(B) 60°

(C) 65°

(D) 70°

Your Answer _____

ANSWERS

A–112

(C) To determine the reciprocal of a fraction, invert it; that is, transpose the numerator and denominator. The reciprocal of 8/5 is 5/8 (choice C). The other answers are incorrect, but notice that choice B is the correct answer to $8 \div 5$. Careful reading is key!

A–113

(D) An isosceles triangle has two equal sides, so the angles opposite the two equal sides are also equal. The question gives the definition when it says "one of the two equal angles." The sum of the three angles in every triangle must equal 180°, so add together the two equal angles and subtract from the total of all three angles: $55 + 55 = 110$; $180 - 110 = 70$ (choice D). Once again, memorize those geometric rules!

QUESTIONS

Q–114

9! is the same as

(A) 9^{10}.

(B) $9 \times 8 \times 7 \times 6 \times 5 \times 4 \times 3 \times 2 \times 1$.

(C) $\sqrt[3]{9}$.

(D) $|9|$.

Your Answer _____

Q–115

A 4-sided pyramid could have a base of which of the following shapes?

(A) Hexagon

(B) Nonagon

(C) Square

(D) Circle

Your Answer _____

ANSWERS

A–114

(B) 9! means 9 factorial, which is expressed as
$9 \times 8 \times 7 \times 6 \times 5 \times 4 \times 3 \times 2 \times 1$. Exponents are
always expressed as numbers, ruling out choice A.
Choices C and D show the cube root of 9 and the absolute
value of 9, respectively; this rules out these choices as well.
So, even if you don't recognize 9!, if you recognize that
the other choices are incorrect, you can deduce the correct
answer, which is B.

A–115

(C) The only shape listed that could be the base of a
4-sided pyramid is a square (choice C). A 4-sided pyramid
must have a base with 4 sides. A 3-sided pyramid would
have a triangular base (3 sides). None of the other answers
is correct.

QUESTIONS

Q–116

Pfcs. Dubois and Kowalski have orders to paint the CO's office. The quartermaster gave them one large container (64 ounces), but they were only able to paint 3/4 of the office. When they go back to supply, the quartermaster has only small (16 ounces) paint containers available. How many small cans do they need to finish the job?

(A) 4

(B) 3

(C) 2

(D) 1

Your Answer _____

Q–117

If $x = 27$, what is the value of $|x - 14|$?

(A) -13

(B) 0

(C) -1

(D) 13

Your Answer _____

ANSWERS

A–116

(C) Let x = the small container and y = the large container. The question tells us that one large container is equal to four small ones, and the privates have already completed 3/4 of the job, so $4x = 3/4y$. To find out how much paint is needed to finish the job, we need to get a value that is $1/4y$. The quantity on the right side of the equation is 3 times the amount we need, so divide by 3: $4/3x = y$; or, $y = 1⅓$. If Pfcs. Dubois and Kowalski need small containers, they need to get two in order to finish the job (choice C).

A–117

(D) Substitute the value for x into the equation: $|27 - 14|$, or $|13|$. This really tests your knowledge of absolute value, which means the value of the number regardless of its sign. $|13|$ is simply 13 (choice D).

QUESTIONS

Q–118

What is the value of $(4)(-3)(1)(-6)$?

(A) 72

(B) -72

(C) -18

(D) 27

Your Answer _____

_____

Q–119

Round off 6,359.218 to the nearest hundredth.

(A) 6,359.21

(B) 6,300

(C) 6,359.2

(D) 6,359.22

Your Answer _____

_____

ANSWERS

A-118

(A) Do the multiplication:

$(4)(-3)(1)(-6)$
$= (-12)(1)(-6)$
$= (-12)(-6) = 72$ (choice A).

Remember the product of two negative numbers is positive!

A-119

(D) "Nearest hundredth" means two digits to the right of the decimal. Because the thousandths digit is greater than 5 (in this case, 8), the rule is to round up the hundredths. 6,359.218 rounded off to the nearest hundredth is 6,359.22 (choice D). Don't forget those basic rules!

QUESTIONS

Q–120

$2.5 \times 10^4 =$

(A) 2,500.

(B) 25,000.

(C) 100.

(D) 10.

Your Answer _____

_____

Q–121

Convert 48% to a fraction (in reduced form).

(A) 1/48

(B) 12/25

(C) 48/100

(D) 1/12

Your Answer _____

_____

ANSWERS

A–120

(B) 2.5×10^4 is a simple multiplication problem; don't be intimidated by exponents. $2.5 \times 10 \times 10 \times 10 \times 10 = 2.5 \times 10,000 = 25,000$ (choice B).

A–121

(B) 48% as a fraction is 48/100. It can be further reduced to 12/25 (4 is a factor of 48 and 100). Because the question specifies "in reduced form," the correct answer is B.

QUESTIONS

Q–122

What is the fraction 45/60 when it is changed to a percentage?

(A) 75%

(B) 33.3%

(C) 66.67%

(D) 25%

Your Answer _____

Q–123

Which symbol means *union* in set theory?

(A) ∩

(B) Ω

(C) ∞

(D) ∪

Your Answer _____

ANSWERS

A–122

(A) First, check to see if the fraction has been reduced. 45/60 can be reduced to 3/4. Once you see a simpler fraction, calculating the percentage is much easier! 3/4 = 75% (choice A). This question tests mathematical ability as well as problem solving, because reducing the fraction is the easiest—and fastest—way to solve this problem. You could also divide and then multiply by 100: 45 ÷ 60 = 0.75 × 100 = 75%.

A–123

(D) In set theory, union is represented by the symbol ∪ (choice D). Choices A, B, and C represent intersection, ohm, and infinity, respectively.

QUESTIONS

Q–124

Which of the following is the closest in shape to a cone?

(A) A megaphone

(B) An umbrella

(C) A parasol

(D) A metronome

Your Answer _____

_____

Q–125

$(x + 3)(x + 4) =$

(A) $x^2 + 7x + 12.$

(B) $x^2 + 12x + 12.$

(C) $x^2 + 12x + 7.$

(D) $x^2 + 7x + 7.$

Your Answer _____

_____

ANSWERS

A–124

(A) A cone is a solid (three-dimensional) object with a circular base and one vertex; the most common everyday example is an ice-cream cone (with a pointy, not smooth, end). Read carefully—the question specifies, "closest in shape." The only choice that would work here is a megaphone, which has a circular base and a vertex of a sort (though the mouthpiece doesn't come to a true point). In any case, the other choices are not cones; don't be fooled by choices B and C, which essentially have the same shape. The correct answer is A.

A–125

(A) First, multiply the first variable in the first set of parentheses by the first variable in the second set of parentheses: $x \times x = x^2$. Next, multiply the first variable in the first set of parentheses with the second number in the second set of parentheses: $x \times 4 = 4x$. Next, multiply the second number in the first set of parentheses by the first variable in the second set of parentheses: $x \times 3 = 3x$. Next, multiply the second number in the first set of parentheses by the second number in the second set parentheses: $3 \times 4 = 12$. Putting it all together: $x^2 + 4x + 3x + 12$. Combine like terms to get the final answer: $x^2 + 7x + 12$ (choice A). The other choices are all incorrect versions of the right answer—choose carefully!

QUESTIONS

Q–126

$\sqrt{625} - \sqrt{256} =$

(A) $\sqrt{369}$.

(B) $\sqrt{81}$.

(C) 9.

(D) Both B and C.

Your Answer _____

Q–127

If the smaller of a pair of supplementary angles $= 45°$, what is the measure of the larger angle in the pair?

(A) 90°

(B) 115°

(C) 135°

(D) 145°

Your Answer _____

ANSWERS

A–126

(D) $25 \times 25 = 625$ and $16 \times 16 = 256$, so $\sqrt{625} - \sqrt{256}$ is the same as $25 - 16 = 9$. However, $9 \times 9 = 81$, so $\sqrt{81} = 9$, meaning choices B and C are both correct. The correct answer is D. Remember that $\sqrt{}$ is the square root (or radical) sign!

A–127

(C) Supplementary angles must equal $180°$, so subtract the measure of the smaller angle ($45°$) to determine the measure of the larger angle in the pair: $180 - 45 = 135$. The larger of the pair of supplementary angles measures $135°$ (choice C).

QUESTIONS

Q–128

Solve the following inequality: $x + 3 \geq 14$.

(A) $x \geq 14$

(B) $x > 14$

(C) $x \geq 11$

(D) $x > 11$

Your Answer _____

Q–129

Which of the following best defines a subtrahend?

(A) An angle that measures less than 180°.

(B) The bottom term in a subtraction expression.

(C) Any part of a circle below the diameter.

(D) The lesser term in an algebraic inequality.

Your Answer _____

ANSWERS

A–128

(C) The statement $x + 3 \geq 14$ means that the x plus 3 is greater than or equal to 14. To solve, isolate x on one side by subtracting 3 from both sides:

$x + 3 - 3 \geq 14 - 3$
$x \geq 11$ (choice C)

To double-check, substitute any number less than or equal to 11 and see if it works: $17 + 3 \geq 14$ (true: $17 + 3 = 20$, which is greater than 14). Solving inequalities can be intimidating, but if you always substitute a number into the solution to see if it works, you can easily see if you solved correctly.

A–129

(B) The last term in a subtraction expression (the number that is being subtracted) is called the *subtrahend* (in $100 - 10$, 10 is the subtrahend). None of the other choices is in any way related; this is just a test of your knowledge of formal mathematical terms. The correct answer is B.

QUESTIONS

Q–130

The only even prime number is ____.

(A) 4

(B) 3

(C) 1

(D) 2

Your Answer _____

_____

ANSWERS

A–130

(D) A prime number is any positive number that is divisible only by two numbers, itself and 1. Thus, the number 2 is the only even prime number. 4 is not prime because it is divisible by 1, 2, and 4. 3 is prime, but not even. 1 is not a prime.

QUESTIONS

Q–131

Succinct most nearly means

(A) talkative.

(B) concise.

(C) passionate.

(D) censored.

Your Answer _____

_____

Q–132

The word *most opposite* in meaning to opulence is

(A) iridescence.

(B) affluence.

(C) luxury.

(D) squalor.

Your Answer _____

_____

ANSWERS

A–131

(B) Be sure to read carefully—the question asks for the word nearest in meaning. *Concise* is nearest in meaning to <u>succinct</u>. *Talkative* is its opposite, and *passionate* is a near opposite; *censored* is in no way related. The correct answer is B.

A–132

(D) Be sure to read carefully—the question asks for the word most opposite in meaning. *Squalor* is opposite in meaning to <u>opulence</u>. *Affluence* and *luxury* are very close in meaning to it; *iridescence* is in no way related. The correct answer is D.

QUESTIONS

Q–133

The surgeon asked for a clamp in order to stop the <u>hemorrhage</u>.

(A) seizure

(B) blood clot

(C) blood loss

(D) paralysis

Your Answer _____

_____

Q–134

<u>Chasm</u> most nearly means

(A) cramp.

(B) vista.

(C) abyss.

(D) mountain.

Your Answer _____

_____

ANSWERS

A–133

(C) Be sure to read the sentence carefully, looking for contextual clues. <u>Hemorrhage</u> means loss, usually one that is significant and sudden. It is often used to describe a loss of blood but can be used in other instances, so *blood loss* is the only choice that would work. The other choices are completely unrelated. The correct answer is C.

A–134

(C) Be sure to read carefully—the question asks for the word nearest in meaning. *Chasm* is nearest in meaning to <u>abyss</u>. *Mountain* is a near opposite, and *vista* and *cramp* are in no way related (except that *chasm* might look like *spasm,* which is close in meaning to *cramp,* if you are reading to quickly!). The correct answer is C.

QUESTIONS

Q–135

Adm. Smarmy exuded <u>charisma</u>, but the seamen were still nervous about the mission.

(A) charm

(B) anger

(C) fear

(D) boredom

Your Answer _____

_____

Q–136

The word *most opposite* in meaning to <u>extol</u> is

(A) laud.

(B) admit.

(C) fail.

(D) demean.

Your Answer _____

_____

ANSWERS

A–135

(A) Be sure to read the sentence carefully, looking for contextual clues. <u>Charisma</u> means "charm." The word *but* indicates that the seamen were nervous in spite of the admiral's demeanor, so he must be the type of person who would not make people feel nervous. Even if you don't know that *charm* is the correct answer, none of the other choices works within the context of the sentence. The correct answer is A.

A–136

(D) Be sure to read carefully—the question asks for the word most opposite in meaning. *Demean* is opposite in meaning to <u>extol</u>. *Laud* is a synonym; the other choices are in no way related. The correct answer is D.

QUESTIONS

Q–137

The proud cadet <u>burnished</u> his medals.

(A) wore

(B) boasted of

(C) polished

(D) heated

Your Answer _____

_____

Q–138

<u>Fiscal</u> most nearly means

(A) bodily.

(B) financial.

(C) annual.

(D) quarterly.

Your Answer _____

_____

ANSWERS

A–137

(C)   Read carefully! Context clues tell you that the cadet is proud of his medals, but <u>burnished</u> does not mean "boasted of"; it means "shined" or "polished" (choice C). Also beware of choices that might seem similar if you don't know the exact meaning—*burnish* might look like *burn* (that is, *heat*), but they are in no way related.

A–138

(B)   Read carefully! <u>Fiscal</u> most nearly means *financial* (choice B). Although *annual* and *quarterly* are related to *fiscal,* they are not even similar in meaning. *Bodily* is in no way related; it is intended to make you misread the word *physical.*

QUESTIONS

Q–139

Brains are a valuable <u>commodity</u>.

(A) asset

(B) skill

(C) trait

(D) possession

Your Answer _____

_____

Q–140

<u>Indigenous</u> most nearly means

(A) naive.

(B) dark blue.

(C) native.

(D) harmless.

Your Answer _____

_____

ANSWERS

A–139

(A) <u>Commodity</u> used in this sense, means *asset* (choice A). It can also mean *product* (as in commodities exchange). Read carefully, but don't be fooled by the fact that brains are also a valuable skill, trait, or possession.

A–140

(C) <u>Indigenous</u> most nearly means *native* (choice C). The other choices are listed to confuse you, because ingenuous, indigo, and innocuous (which are the meanings of choices A, B, and D, respectively) might "look like" *indigenous* if you don't read carefully.

QUESTIONS

Q–141

In addition to being a well-respected officer,
Gen. Gourmand was a <u>connoisseur</u> of French cuisine.

(A) aficionado

(B) glutton

(C) chef

(D) server

Your Answer _____

_____

Q–142

<u>Blasphemy</u> most nearly means

(A) flattery.

(B) curse.

(C) sacrilege.

(D) holy.

Your Answer _____

_____

ANSWERS

A–141

(A) <u>Connoisseur</u> means expert judge of quality (of food, art, music, etc.). *Aficionado* means nearly the same thing. A *glutton* is someone who overeats (or does anything to excess); a *chef* is a trained cook; a *server* is the person in a restaurant who brings guests their food and beverages. The correct answer is A.

A–142

(C) <u>Blasphemy</u> means an insult to something held sacred or holy. *Sacrilege* means nearly the same thing. A *curse* could be a form of blasphemy, but it is not truly near it in meaning; *flattery* is in no way related in meaning. The correct answer is C.

QUESTIONS

Q–143

The word *most opposite* in meaning to <u>pauper</u> is

(A) billionaire

(B) monk

(C) entrepreneur

(D) trendsetter

Your Answer _____

_____

Q–144

<u>Zenith</u> most nearly means

(A) nadir.

(B) apex.

(C) crux.

(D) plateau.

Your Answer _____

_____

ANSWERS

A–143

(A) A <u>pauper</u> is a very poor person; the most opposite of which from the choices given would be *billionaire* (choice A). Although many monastic orders take vows of poverty, a *monk* is not necessarily a pauper. An *entrepreneur* is a self-made businessperson, usually one who launched an innovative product or idea. *Trendsetters* are people who ignore prevailing ideas and/or styles, opting instead to blaze their own trail (sometimes they are called trailblazers).

A–144

(B) <u>Zenith</u> means highest point; the word closest to it in meaning among the choices given is *apex* (other good synonyms include *summit* and *acme*). *Nadir,* the opposite of *zenith,* means lowest point. *Crux* means essential point. *Plateau* means an area of flat land (it is also used to mean that something has reached a "flat" point, as when a dieter cannot lose additional weight despite increased effort). The correct answer is B.

QUESTIONS

Q–145

The word *most opposite* in meaning to <u>dearth</u> is

(A) health.

(B) vitality.

(C) scarcity.

(D) plethora.

Your Answer _____

_____

Q–146

Cpl. Workman's medal told fellow soldiers she <u>epitomized</u> bravery.

(A) admired

(B) typified

(C) strove for

(D) dressed for

Your Answer _____

_____

ANSWERS

A–145

(D) <u>Dearth</u> means *scarcity* (ruling out choice C). *Health* and *vitality* have nothing to do with dearth; they are included to confuse you because if you don't read carefully, dearth might look like death. *Plethora,* however, means abundance or plenty, which is the opposite of dearth, and so, the correct answer (choice D).

A–146

(B) <u>Epitomize</u> means to symbolize or be a typical representation of something; the *epitome* is the "ultimate example" or the "last word." *Typify* is a synonym for *epitomize*; *admire* and *dress for* are not. To *strive* means in the process of attempting—one who strives for bravery would not already have a medal. The correct answer is B.

QUESTIONS

Q–147

<u>Circuitous</u> most nearly means

(A) electrical.

(B) direct.

(C) complete.

(D) rambling.

Your Answer _____

_____

Q–148

The word *most opposite* in meaning to <u>rudimentary</u> is

(A) polite

(B) basic

(C) advanced

(D) essential

Your Answer _____

_____

ANSWERS

A–147

(D) <u>Circuitous</u> means roundabout or indirect. The closest in meaning to it would be *rambling* (choice D). Another good synonym would be *meandering. Direct* is opposite in meaning. *Electrical* and *complete* are not related to it in meaning—do not be confused by the fact that they are related to circuits. The correct answer is D.

A–148

(C) <u>Rudimentary</u> means basic or fundamental, which rules out choice B as an antonym of it. The word most opposite in meaning to it is *advanced.* Neither *polite* nor *essential* are correct choices for antonyms of *rudimentary,* which has nothing to do with being rude or unnecessary, the opposites of each of those words, respectively. The correct answer is C.

QUESTIONS

Q–149

Innate most nearly means

(A) inborn.

(B) taught.

(C) artificial.

(D) creative.

Your Answer _____

_____

Q–150

Umbrage most nearly means

(A) discourtesy.

(B) pleasure.

(C) fault.

(D) offense.

Your Answer _____

_____

ANSWERS

A–149

(A) <u>Innate</u> means native or *inborn* (choice A). None of the other choices is close in meaning to *innate*.

A–150

(D) <u>Umbrage</u> means resentment or *offense* (choice D). *Pleasure* would be a good antonym for *umbrage*. *Fault* and *discourtesy* are not synonyms for it, but one could take umbrage at another's faults or discourtesy. The correct answer is D.

QUESTIONS

Q–151

Self-esteem is <u>intrinsic</u> to success in life.

(A) unnecessary

(B) essential

(C) unnatural

(D) unrelated

Your Answer _____

_____

Q–152

The word *most opposite* in meaning to <u>malign</u> is

(A) slander.

(B) predict.

(C) praise.

(D) plead.

Your Answer _____

_____

ANSWERS

A–151

(B) <u>Intrinsic</u> means natural or *essential* to (choice B). *Unnecessary* and *unnatural* would be good antonyms for it. Context should help you determine that *unrelated* does not fit the sentence, ruling out choice D. The correct answer is B.

A–152

(C) <u>Malign</u> means to speak ill of or to defame. *Slander* would be a good synonym for *malign*; *predict* and *plead* are neither good synonyms nor good antonyms for it. However, *praise* is opposite in meaning to *malign*. The correct answer is C.

QUESTIONS

Q–153

The CO called the company clerk a <u>paragon</u> of efficiency.

(A) model

(B) contradiction

(C) pattern

(D) devotée

Your Answer _____

_____

Q–154

<u>Dissension</u> most nearly means

(A) swelling.

(B) harmony.

(C) conflict.

(D) agreement.

Your Answer _____

_____

ANSWERS

A–153

(A) A <u>paragon</u> is a shining example or an ideal. The best choice given as a synonym for it is *model* (choice A). *Contradiction* is close in meaning to *paradox*, but not *paragon*; likewise, *pattern* is close in meaning to *paradigm*, but not *paragon*—both choices are included to confuse you. *Devotée* is in no way related to *paragon*. The correct answer is A.

A–154

(C) <u>Dissension</u> means discord or disagreement. The word closest to it in meaning is *conflict* (choice C). Other good synonyms would be *discord*, *strife,* and *flak*. *Harmony* and *agreement* are both opposite in meaning to it. *Swelling* is close in meaning to *distension*, not *dissension*. One letter can cause you to pick the wrong answer when you're under pressure, so always make sure you read carefully. The correct answer is C.

QUESTIONS

Q–155

Platitude most nearly means

(A) banality.

(B) serving dish.

(C) wisdom.

(D) slogan.

Your Answer _____

_____

Q–156

Imperative most nearly means

(A) haughty.

(B) obligatory.

(C) royal.

(D) bold.

Your Answer _____

_____

ANSWERS

A–155

(A) A <u>platitude</u> is a common expression that has become trite from overuse. Of the choices listed, *banality* is closest to it in meaning (choice A); another good synonym for it is *cliché*. A *serving dish* would be a good synonym for *platter*. *Wisdom* is not a synonym for *platitude*. A *slogan* (motto or catchphrase), though not a synonym, can become a platitude if overused. The correct answer is A.

A–156

(B) <u>Imperative</u> means urgent or mandatory. *Obligatory* is closest to it in meaning among the choices listed. *Haughty* and *royal* would be good synonyms for *imperious* and *imperial*, respectively, but not for *imperative*. *Bold* is not related in meaning. The correct answer is B.

QUESTIONS

Q–157

The word *most opposite* in meaning to <u>boon</u> is

(A) disaster.

(B) quiet.

(C) depression.

(D) benefit.

Your Answer _____

Q–158

The major's pre-mission speech warned the company that <u>camouflage</u> of themselves and their equipment was key to safe and successful recon.

(A) maintenance

(B) exposure

(C) development

(D) concealment

Your Answer _____

ANSWERS

A–157

(A) A <u>boon</u> is something helpful or beneficial, so *benefit* is a synonym, not an antonym, ruling out choice D. *Quiet* and *depression* would be good synonyms for *boom*, but not for *boon*. However, *disaster* is opposite in meaning to *boon,* which makes the correct answer A.

A–158

(D) <u>Camouflage</u> is the use of disguise to make something harder to see. A good synonym for it would be *concealment. Exposure* is opposite in meaning, and *development* and *maintenance* are not at all related. The correct answer is D. "Recon" is a contextual clue—to be safe and successful, the soldiers and their equipment would need to be concealed.

QUESTIONS

Q–159

Telemetry most nearly means

(A) long-distance communication.

(B) mental communication.

(C) audacity or rash behavior.

(D) transmission of measurements by automatic instruments.

Your Answer _____

Q–160

Criterion most nearly means

(A) judgment.

(B) standard.

(C) excerpt.

(D) ruler.

Your Answer _____

ANSWERS

A–159

(D) <u>Telemetry</u> is the transmission of measurements by automatic instruments (choice D); it is commonly used in hospitals to measure cardiac function, among other medical applications. Choice A might be a good definition for *telephony*; choice B would be a good definition for *telepathy*; choice C contains two synonyms for *temerity*. The correct answer is D. Because *temerity* is not a common word, the other choices are listed to trick you into picking a choice that would work with one of them; if you read carefully, you know none of them is the word in the question, and you can simply rule them out one by one.

A–160

(B) A <u>criterion</u> is something that a judgment can be based on. The closest to it in meaning would be *standard* (*touchstone* and *benchmark* are good synonyms, too). *Judgment* is not a synonym for it; neither is *ruler* (but *yardstick*, used in the figurative sense, is). *Excerpt* is in no way related to *criterion*. The correct answer is B. Note that it often appears in the plural: *criteria.*

QUESTIONS

Q–161

Articulate most nearly means

(A) well-spoken.

(B) well-groomed.

(C) well-mannered.

(D) attractive.

Your Answer _____

_____

Q–162

Throughout much of history Christmas Day was considered sacrosanct, and soldiers on both sides lay down their weapons.

(A) a cease-fire

(B) holy

(C) sacrilegious

(D) profane

Your Answer _____

_____

ANSWERS

A–161

(A) <u>Articulate</u> means well-spoken (choice A).

The other choices are not synonyms, although the ability to speak well is certainly a positive trait that others may find attractive. A good synonym for *articulate* is *eloquent.* The correct answer is A.

A–162

(B) Something <u>sacrosanct</u> is held sacred. The choice listed that is closest in meaning is *holy* (choice B). *Sacrilegious* and *profane* are opposite in meaning to *sacrosanct,* and *cease-fire* is not related. "Christmas Day" is the contextual clue that should lead you to the correct answer (choice B).

QUESTIONS

Q–163

When they reached the shoreline of the enemy's island
<u>bastion</u>, the marines nodded to each other in silent victory.

(A) stronghold

(B) cache

(C) hideout

(D) training ground

Your Answer ———————————————————

Q–164

The sudden <u>silhouette</u> in the moonlit jungle made the sentry
grip his rifle, but it was only the corporal who was his relief.

(A) bright light

(B) rustling

(C) outline

(D) sharp noise

Your Answer ———————————————————

ANSWERS

A–163

(A) <u>Bastion</u> means fortress or fortified area, to which *stronghold* is close in meaning. A *cache* (stockpile), *hideout,* and *training ground* all could be parts of a bastion, but are not synonyms for it. The correct answer is A.

A–164

(C) A <u>silhouette</u> is a contour or *outline* (choice C). There are no significant contextual clues here if you don't know the meaning of the word. Artistically, silhouettes are outline drawings done in black, usually of people posed in profile. Thinking of that image can help you remember the meaning. The correct answer is C.

QUESTIONS

Q–165

The word *most opposite* in meaning to <u>curtail</u> is

(A) extend.

(B) abrupt.

(C) reduce.

(D) speed.

Your Answer _____

Q–166

<u>Deportment</u> most nearly means

(A) exile.

(B) location.

(C) behavior.

(D) timeliness.

Your Answer _____

ANSWERS

A–165

(A) <u>Curtail</u> means cut short or *reduce*. The most opposite in meaning to it among the choices listed is *extend*. *Abrupt* is a synonym for *curt*, and *speed* is not related in meaning. The correct answer is A.

A–166

(C) <u>Deportment</u> means conduct, manner, bearing, etc. *Behavior* is a good synonym (choice C). Deportment has nothing to do with deportation, so *exile* is in no way related; neither is *location* nor *timeliness*. The correct answer is C.

QUESTIONS

Q–167

<u>Mercurial</u> most nearly means

(A) unpredictable.

(B) constant.

(C) metallic.

(D) quicksilver.

Your Answer _____

Q–168

<u>Picayune</u> most nearly means

(A) spicy.

(B) obsessive.

(C) trivial.

(D) detailed.

Your Answer _____

ANSWERS

A–167

(A) Someone who is <u>mercurial</u> lacks stability and has swiftly changing moods; closest in meaning to it among the choices given is *unpredictable* (other good synonyms are *capricious* and *fickle*). *Constant* is the opposite of *mercurial*; the element mercury is *metallic* and *quicksilver* is another name for it. The correct answer is A.

A–168

(C) <u>Picayune</u> means insignificant or petty. Closest to it in meaning is *trivial*. *Spicy* would be a synonym for *piquant*, not *picayune*. *Obsessive* and *detailed* are not really related to *picayune*. (Note that *picayune* is often used to describe perfectionists and sticklers for detail, but this is incorrect usage unless these are people who pore over insignificant minutiae or obsess needlessly; in other words, such individuals are not picayune themselves, nor are their findings necessarily picayune, per se.) The correct answer is C.

QUESTIONS

Q–169

The ship's doctor advised the commander to <u>eschew</u> fried foods until his digestion improved.

(A) abstain from

(B) indulge in

(C) eat more of

(D) prepare

Your Answer _____

_____

Q–170

The press was out in full force to cover the <u>plenary</u> session of Congress.

(A) full

(B) emergency

(C) newsworthy

(D) scheduled

Your Answer _____

_____

ANSWERS

A–169

(A) <u>Eschew</u> means to avoid or stay away from. Of the choices listed, the best is *abstain from* (choice A). *Indulge in* or *eat more of* would be the opposite of *eschew*. *Prepare* is in no way related. Contextually, you can determine that the answer should be something close in meaning to *avoid*, as doctors usually do not encourage patients to eat fried food. Even if *eschew* and *abstain* are not in your vocabulary, you can rule out the others. The correct answer is A.

A–170

(A) <u>Plenary</u> means *full* (think of plenty). The other choices, though they could make sense in the context of the sentence, are not related in meaning to *plenary*. This is simply a word you need to know or deduce. The correct answer is A.

QUESTIONS

Q–171

Although he did not really sanction their decision, their CO gave the noncoms his <u>tacit</u> approval.

(A) unqualified

(B) unspoken

(C) written

(D) stamped

Your Answer _____

Q–172

The word *most opposite* in meaning to <u>insouciant</u> is

(A) bubbly.

(B) willful.

(C) defiant.

(D) glum.

Your Answer _____

ANSWERS

A–171

(B) <u>Tacit</u> means silent. Of the choices given, *unspoken* is closest in meaning. Because the sentence specifies "Although he did not really sanction their decision," *unqualified* does not make sense. *Written* or *stamped,* would not be likely either, given the context. The correct answer is B. (Another word related to tacit is *taciturn,* which means "of few words": *Their father was a <u>taciturn</u> man, and so when he did speak, people paid attention.*)

A–172

(D) <u>Insouciant</u> means happy-go-lucky. Its nearest opposite is *glum. Bubbly,* like its synonym, *effervescent,* is close in meaning to *insouciant. Willful* and *defiant,* though close in meaning to each other, are neither synonyms nor antonyms of *insouciant.* The correct answer is D.

QUESTIONS

Q–173

The word *most opposite* in meaning to <u>equivocate</u> is

(A) lose one's balance.

(B) speak plainly.

(C) muffle.

(D) treat unfairly.

Your Answer _____

Q–174

Because she was a <u>polyglot</u>, Sgt. Lingua went to work for the UN after completing her tour of duty.

(A) diplomat

(B) peacekeeper

(C) lover of travel

(D) speaker of many languages

Your Answer _____

ANSWERS

A–173

(B) To *equivocate* means to hedge or sidestep (*evade* is a good synonym); of the choices given, the most opposite in meaning is *speak plainly* (choice B). The other choices are in no way related in meaning to *equivocate*. The correct answer is B.

A–174

(D) A <u>polyglot</u> is someone who speaks many languages, so choice D is correct. The other choices are not related to *polyglot*. This is a question where only knowing the word—or recognizing its components—will help you get the right answer. *Diplomat, peacekeeper,* and *lover of travel* all could make sense contextually because of the reference to the UN. However, if you know that *poly* means "many" and *glot* (also, *gloss*) means "language or tongue," this suddenly becomes an easy word instead of a stumper! (Other *poly* and *glot* words include *polymath*—person of encyclopedic learning—and *glottochronology*—the study of the history/development of languages.)

QUESTIONS

Q–175

<u>Ephemeral</u> most nearly means

(A) transitory.

(B) slender.

(C) silky.

(D) effective.

Your Answer _____

_____

Q–176

<u>Mulct</u> most nearly means

(A) complaint.

(B) multiple.

(C) penalty.

(D) fertilizer.

Your Answer _____

_____

ANSWERS

A–175

(A) <u>Ephemeral</u> means lasting only a short time; of the choices given, the one closest in meaning is *transitory* (other good synonyms are *short-lived, transient, evanescent*). The other choices are in no way related to *ephemeral*. The correct answer is A. (Note that because fads are ephemeral, *faddish* is sometimes mistakenly used as a synonym; however, everything that is ephemeral is not necessarily a fad, but it is necessarily short-lived.)

A–176

(C) <u>Mulct</u> means fine or penalty (choice C). The other choices do not relate to *mulct* in any way. Read carefully— the word is *mulct,* not *mulch,* which is a type of material used in landscaping and so could be misinterpreted as meaning *fertilize.* The correct answer is C.

QUESTIONS

Q–177

Proclivity most nearly means

(A) disinclination.

(B) predilection.

(C) aversion.

(D) perversion.

Your Answer _____

_____

Q–178

The word *most opposite* in meaning to gibbous is

(A) bright.

(B) greasy.

(C) flat.

(D) smooth.

Your Answer _____

_____

ANSWERS

A–177

(B) <u>Proclivity</u> means inclination or tendency. The choice nearest to it in meaning is *predilection* (choice B). *Disinclination* and *aversion* are both antonyms of it, and *perversion* is not related to it in meaning. The correct answer is B.

A–178

(C) <u>Gibbous</u> means convex, swollen, or distended; in reference to planets or the moon, it means that more than half, but not all, of the celestial body is illuminated (a gibbous moon is between a half moon and a full moon). Closest in meaning is *flat*; the other choices are not related to *gibbous*. The correct answer is C.

QUESTIONS

Q–179

The woman was touched more by her husband's words than by the <u>panoply</u> of flowers he gave her.

(A) display

(B) bouquet

(C) vista

(D) apology

Your Answer _____

Q–180

The word *most opposite* in meaning to <u>lackadaisical</u> is

(A) shiny.

(B) industrious.

(C) fawning.

(D) plain.

Your Answer _____

ANSWERS

A–179

(A) A <u>panoply</u> is an impressive array of something; the choice closest in meaning is *display* (choice A). *Bouquet, vista,* and *apology* are not related in meaning to *panoply*. If you have no idea what *panoply* means, *bouquet* could seem correct because of the mention of flowers. *Vista* would be a synonym for *panorama,* not *panoply*. Contextually, *apology* would not make sense because the sentence specifies that "the woman was touched more by her husband's words," so the words, not the flowers, would be the apology. The correct answer is A. Vocabulary building is something you just need to do in order to do well on this part of the test.

A–180

(B) <u>Lackadaisical</u> means listless or lazy. Of the choices given, the word most opposite in meaning is *industrious* (choice B). *Shiny* would be an antonym for *lackluster,* not *lackadaisical*. Someone who is *fawning* is called a lackey. *Plain* is in no way related in meaning. The correct answer is B.

QUESTIONS

Q–181

Weal most nearly means

(A) sob.

(B) train.

(C) ardor.

(D) prosperity.

Your Answer _____

Q–182

Limn most nearly means

(A) aquatic.

(B) straight.

(C) delineated.

(D) citrus.

Your Answer _____

ANSWERS

A–181

(D) <u>Weal</u> means prosperous state or well-being (it is of the same root as *wealth*). Of the choices listed, *prosperity* is the closest in meaning. *Sob* is close in meaning to *wail*, *train* is close in meaning to *wean,* and *ardor* is close in meaning to *zeal*. The correct answer is D. (Note that a secondary meaning of *weal* is welt or swelling.)

A–182

(C) <u>Limn</u> means to paint or draw or outline. Of the choices listed, *delineate* is closest in meaning (choice C). Limn is related to lines, but *straight* is not the best answer; however, limn has nothing to with limes, ruling out *citrus*. It is in no way related in meaning to *aquatic* (although limnology is the study of freshwater habitats). The correct answer is C.

QUESTIONS

Q–183

Illusive most nearly means

(A) evasive.

(B) slippery.

(C) well-lit.

(D) deceptive.

Your Answer _____

_____

Q–184

The word *most opposite* in meaning to subterfuge is

(A) above ground.

(B) sandwich.

(C) ruse.

(D) honesty.

Your Answer _____

_____

ANSWERS

A–183

(D) Illusive means imaginary or false; the choice closest in meaning to it is *deceptive* (choice D) and the two are commonly used synonymously. Both *evasive* and *slippery* could be used as synonyms for *elusive,* with which *illusive* is commonly confused—always read carefully, and double-check the word sought in the question. *Well-lit* is close in meaning to *illuminated,* but not *illusive.* The correct answer is D.

A–184

(D) A subterfuge is a deception or the concealment of one's true activities or intentions. *Ruse* would be a good synonym for *subterfuge.* However, the word most opposite in meaning to *subterfuge* from among the choices given is *honesty* (choice D). *Above ground* (antonym for *subterranean*) and *sandwich* (as in "sub") are not in any way related to *subterfuge.* The correct answer is D.

QUESTIONS

Q–185

The word *most opposite* in meaning to <u>aperçu</u> is

(A) cocktail.

(B) sketch.

(C) saga.

(D) summary.

Your Answer _____

_____

Q–186

The word *most opposite* in meaning to <u>fallacious</u> is

(A) fanciful.

(B) accurate.

(C) invalid.

(D) jocund.

Your Answer _____

_____

ANSWERS

A–185

(C) An <u>aperçu</u> is a brief outline or overview; *sketch* or *summary* would be synonymous, not antonymous, with it. An apéritif is another word for a *cocktail.* Because it means long, detailed, drawn-out story or account, *saga* is the best choice as an antonym for *aperçu.* The correct answer is C.

A–186

(B) <u>Fallacious</u> means false or imaginary (it is the adjectival form of *fallacy*). The nearest opposite to *fallacious* here is *accurate* (choice B). *Fanciful* and *invalid* (in the sense of "not valid," not "chronically ill person") would be good synonyms for *fallacious. Jocund* would be a good synonym for *facetious,* not *fallacious.* The correct answer is B.

QUESTIONS

Q–187

Col. Icarus stood at attention as the general described many moments from the <u>illustrious</u> career of the Air Force colonel.

(A) impressive

(B) long

(C) colorful

(D) deplorable

Your Answer _____

_____

Q–188

The pastor looked at the few coins on the collection plate and wondered how his small church was supposed to survive as an <u>eleemosynary</u> institution.

(A) fundamental

(B) community

(C) eccesiastical

(D) charitable

Your Answer _____

_____

ANSWERS

A–187

(A) <u>Illustrious</u> means famous or distinguished, so closest to it in meaning of the choices listed is *impressive* (choice A). Both *long* and *colorful* could apply to *illustrious,* but are not synonymous with it (*colorful* is actually there to be confused with *illustrated*). *Deplorable* is a good synonym for *ignoble* or *ignominious,* not *illustrious.* The correct answer is A.

A–188

(D) An <u>eleemosynary</u> institution is one supported by alms or charity. Closest to it in meaning is *charitable* (choice D). *Fundamental, community,* and *ecclesiastical* are not related to it in meaning, although they could seem correct from context alone. When you come across a "stumper" like this one, look for contextual clues. In this case, it is "few coins on the collection plate," which indicates that charitable support is insufficient. The correct answer is D.

QUESTIONS

Q–189

The word *most opposite* in meaning to <u>autochthonous</u> is

(A) indigenous.

(B) foreign.

(C) dependent.

(D) voluntary.

Your Answer _____

Q–190

<u>Acquiesce</u> most nearly means

(A) yield.

(B) rest.

(C) obtain.

(D) cease.

Your Answer _____

ANSWERS

A–189

(B) <u>Autochthonous</u> means native or indigenous.
Indigenous would be a synonym, not an antonym, ruling
it out as correct in this case. *Dependent* and *voluntary*
would be good antonyms for *autonomous* and *automatic,*
respectively, but not for *autochthonous*. The correct answer
is B. (If you break down its component parts—*auto* [self]
and *chthonos* [earth]—you can see that it literally means
"of its own soil," that is, native or indigenous. In any case,
you can add it to your official list of "big words"! Great for
crossword puzzles. . . .)

A–190

(A) <u>Acquiesce</u> means to give in (to a request or demand).
Of the choices listed, the one closest in meaning is
yield (choice A). None of the other choices are related
in meaning to *acquiesce,* but *obtain* would be close in
meaning to *acquire*. The correct answer is A.

QUESTIONS

Q–191

<u>Purview</u> most nearly means

(A) perspective.

(B) compromise.

(C) jurisdiction.

(D) proviso.

Your Answer _____

Q–192

The generals gathered in the war room to discuss the <u>strategy</u> for the upcoming battle.

(A) trick

(B) tactic

(C) weaponry

(D) game

Your Answer _____

ANSWERS

A–191

(C) <u>Purview</u> means range of authority or responsibility. From among the choices listed, *jurisdiction* is closest in meaning. *Perspective* (viewpoint), *compromise* (give-and-take), and *proviso* (requirement) are related in meaning to *purview*. The correct answer is C.

A–192

(B) A <u>strategy</u> is a plan or *tactic* (choice B). Although another term for strategy is *game plan,* and trickery can be part of a strategy, neither *game* nor *trick* are synonyms for it. (*Trick* is a synonym for *stratagem*.) *Weaponry* is not a synonym for *strategy* either, but weapons are part of battle strategy. The correct answer is B.

QUESTIONS

Q–193

The word *most opposite* in meaning to <u>inscrutable</u> is

(A) obvious.

(B) enigmatic.

(C) principled.

(D) criminal.

Your Answer _____

_____

Q–194

<u>Quell</u> most nearly means

(A) slake.

(B) doubt.

(C) extinguish.

(D) vanquish.

Your Answer _____

_____

ANSWERS

A–193

(A) <u>Inscrutable</u> means unknowable, mysterious, or hard to read (as in a person's facial expression). The closest opposite would be *obvious* (choice A); a good synonym would be *enigmatic. Principled* and *criminal* would be good as a synonym and antonym, respectively, for *unscrupulous,* but not for *inscrutable.* Read carefully! The correct answer is A.

A–194

(D) <u>Quell</u> means subdue or conquer; *vanquish* is an excellent synonym (choice D). *Slake* and *extinguish* would be good synonyms for the two meanings of *quench,* but not for *quell. Doubt* would be a good synonym for *qualm,* not *quell.* The correct answer is D.

QUESTIONS

Q–195

Spate most nearly means

(A) argument.

(B) hoe.

(C) extra.

(D) outpouring.

Your Answer _____

_____

ANSWERS

A–195

(D) <u>Spate</u> means flood or inundation (it is frequently used figuratively, as in "a spate of tears"). Closest to it in meaning is *outpouring* (choice D). This is another instance where careful reading is key, as the other choices could appear to be correct for spat (*argument*), spade (*hoe*) or spare (*extra*). The correct answer is D.

QUESTIONS

In addition to its metallic properties, silver is an antimicrobial. Now used as a component of topical antibiotics, scientists and historians speculate that wealthy people did not succumb to the Black Death (bubonic plague) that decimated much of the population in 14th-century (1300s) Europe because they primarily ate with utensils, plates, and drinking vessels made of silver.

Q–196

From the passage we can infer that:

(A) Silver is not a metal.

(B) The bubonic plague killed half the people living in Europe.

(C) Silver can prevent infection because it has antimicrobial properties.

(D) There were a lot of wealthy people in Europe during the 1300s.

Your Answer _____

_____

ANSWERS

A–196

(C) According to the passage, silver is a metal with antimicrobial properties, leading current scientists and historians to think it prevented wealthy people from contracting bubonic plague during the Black Death of the 1300s, which destroyed much of Europe's population. "Half" the population implies a specific number, as opposed to "much," which does not. It is implied that there were not many wealthy people in Europe at that time; otherwise, "much of the population" would not have died. The correct answer is C.

QUESTIONS

Use the following passage to answer questions 197 and 198.

Flowers contain both male and female parts, which is why most of them require insects, such as bees, for pollination. In this process, pollen is transferred from the male parts (stamen and anther), where it is produced, to the female parts (pistil and stigma) so that fertilization can occur, eventually resulting in new plant growth.

Q–197

According to the passage:

(A)   The pistil is a female part of flowers.

(B)   Pollen is produced in the stigma of the flower.

(C)   The anther is a female part of the flower.

(D)   Pollination does not cause new plants to grow.

Your Answer _____

_____

Q–198

The passage supports which statement(s)?

(A)   The stamen is not involved in pollination.

(B)   Fertilization is achieved by pollination.

(C)   Bees often enable pollination by transferring pollen.

(D)   B and C, but not A.

Your Answer _____

_____

ANSWERS

A–197

(A) According to the passage, the only choice containing correct information is choice A. All the other choices state the opposite of what the passage states. Read all passages carefully, and then check the answer choices against them, rather than trying to recall what you might know about the topic.

A–198

(D) Reading carefully is especially important when the instructions specify that two answers will be derived from one passage. The passage supports B and C, but not A; thus, the correct answer is D.

QUESTIONS

The Third Infantry Regiment ("Old Guard") is responsible for providing ceremonial units and honor guards for state occasions, White House social functions, public celebrations and interments at Arlington National Cemetery—as well as standing a very formal sentry watch at the Tomb of the Unknowns, where visitors can stand to observe the guards and their measured steps and silent, almost mechanical, rifle shoulder changes. Each guard takes 21 steps during his march across the area around the tomb; these steps allude to the 21-gun salute, which is the highest honor given to any military or foreign dignitary. Each guard also pauses for 21 seconds before changing direction, for the same reason. Guards are changed every 30 minutes, 24 hours a day, 365 days a year—regardless of the weather—just as the tomb has been continuously guarded since 1930.

Q–199

According to the passage:

(A) The Third Infantry Regiment provides the guards for the Tomb of the Unknowns and also provides honor guards for state occasions.

(B) Guards are changed every 30 minutes round the clock, but the tomb is not patrolled during storms.

(C) The guards' 21 steps and 21-second pauses prior to changing direction are related to the 21-gun salute.

(D) A and C, but not B.

Your Answer _____

_____

ANSWERS

A–199

(D) According to the passage, the Third Infantry Regiment provides the guards for the Tomb of the Unknowns, and also provides honor guards for state occasions; guards are changed every 30 minutes round the clock, regardless of the weather; and the guards' 21 steps and 21-second pauses prior to changing direction are related to the 21-gun salute. Therefore, all the information in choices A and C is true, but not all the information in choice B is true—guards are changed every 30 seconds round the clock, and the tomb is patrolled during storms. The contextual clue is "regardless of the weather." The correct answer is D.

QUESTIONS

Use the following passage to answer questions 200 and 201.

The concept of opposites that exist in a delicate balance—yin and yang—permeates both ancient and contemporary Chinese thought. These opposing yet complementary forces are believed to pervade not just the earth, but the entire universe. Yin is associated with female, absorbing qualities (passivity, darkness, and the moon); yang is linked to male, penetrating qualities (activity, brightness, and the sun). This extends to all things: In the realm of beasts, yin is the tiger, and yang is the dragon; in landscape, valleys are yin, and mountains are yang; broken lines and even numbers are yin, while unbroken lines and odd numbers are yang. The two qualities are in constant fluctuation, with one giving way as the other expands—thus, light becomes dark, and heat turns to cold. This interaction is believed to be the very process that balances all life.

Q–200

According to the beliefs discussed in this passage:

(A) Dragons symbolize yin.

(B) Yin and yang permeate the entire universe.

(C) All numbers contain yang qualities.

(D) Brightness and the sun are associated with yin.

Your Answer _____

_____

ANSWERS

A–200

(B) According to the beliefs discussed in this passage, yin and yang permeate the entire universe (choice B). However, dragons symbolize yang, not yin; yang numbers represent only odd numbers; brightness and the sun are associated with yang, not yin. The correct answer is B.

QUESTIONS

Q–201

<u>Pervade</u>, as used in this passage, means

(A) corrupt.

(B) weaken.

(C) penetrate.

(D) empty.

Your Answer _____

ANSWERS

A–201

(C) <u>Pervade</u> means "to spread throughout." The closest in meaning to it from among the choices listed is *penetrate* (choice C). *Corrupt* would be a good synonym for perverse; *empty* and *weaken* are close opposites to <u>pervade</u>. The correct answer is C.

QUESTIONS

Billions of years ago, algae began transforming the carbon dioxide in the atmosphere into the oxygen-rich world that makes life on earth possible. Blue-green algae can be thought of as the great-great-great-grandparents of well over 30,000 different species of algae. Many people believe that decades of chemical farming practices have leached American soils, causing them to lack some very important nutrients. As a result, eating some form of algae is important to maintain good health. Those most informed about phytonutrients consider blue-green algae, which still grows wild, to be the best form.

Q–202

The author of this passage would agree that:

(A) Eating the phytonutrients found in blue-green algae is necessary to maintaining good health.

(B) Blue-green algae consumed today are related to the blue-green algae of billions of years ago.

(C) People can obtain all the nutrients they need from food grown in the United States.

(D) A and B, but not C.

Your Answer _____

ANSWERS

A–202

(D) The author of the passage specifies that algae consumption is necessary to good health and that blue-green algae is the best form, so he/she would agree with choice A; blue-green algae is further described as the "great-great-great-grandparents of well over 30,000 different species of algae" and it is also stated that it "still grows wild," so he/she would agree with choice B. However, the statement is made that "chemical farming practices have leached American soils, causing them to lack some very important nutrients . . . eating some form of algae is important to maintain good health"; so he/she would not agree with choice C. Thus, the correct answer must be D.

QUESTIONS

In 1902, Joseph V. Horn and Frank Hardart opened the first Automat in Philadelphia, Pennsylvania; more followed throughout the Mid-Atlantic states. The Automat was famous for the buns, beans, and fish cakes made fresh every day and stored behind small glass windows that could be opened by inserting coins into each accompanying slot. Low prices caused these eateries to become extremely popular during the Great Depression. In the 1940s and 1950s, upward of 300,000 people were served daily. Automats were successful until the 1960s, when "fast food" began luring customers away.

Q–203

According to the passage, which of the following is true about Automats?

(A) They were successful because of their friendly waitstaff.

(B) In difficult economic times, low prices did not impact their popularity.

(C) They are still popular today.

(D) Patrons needed to insert coins into a slot to obtain their food.

Your Answer _____

_____

ANSWERS

(D) The passage clearly states that food was behind glass windows and coins needed to be inserted into a slot to obtain the food (choice D). No mention is made of waitstaff, ruling out choice A. The passage specifies that low prices made the Automat popular during the Great Depression but that "fast food" ended its popularity (context clue: "luring away customers") in the 1960s, ruling out choices B and C. The correct answer is D.

QUESTIONS

Use the following passage to answer questions 204 and 205.

For almost four centuries, the Topkapi Palace in Constantinople (modern-day Istanbul, Turkey) was the center of a splendid empire. Foreign ambassadors from both the East and West waited anxiously to be presented to the "Shadow of God on Earth," the Ottoman sultan who ruled subjects in Asia, Europe, and Africa. Those who were honored by being invited to enter the public areas of the Topkapi found a marvelous assembly of costumed courtiers and military guards, as well as an incredible display of gold, jewels, colorful carpets, and impressive armor and weaponry. Only the sultan and his family could enter the *harem* (meaning "private area") of the palace, where the royals lived in unparalleled luxury. Today the Topkapi is a renowned museum, with exhibits that tour worldwide.

Q–204

As described in the passage:

(A) The Topkapi, formerly a palace, is now a museum.

(B) The *harem* was the part of the palace where foreign dignitaries were entertained.

(C) The Ottoman empire extended across three continents.

(D) A and C, but not B.

Your Answer _____

ANSWERS

A–204

(D) As described in the passage, the Topkapi, the palace of the Ottoman sultans (an empire that lasted almost 400 years), is now a museum and the Ottoman empire extended across three continents (Asia, Europe, and Africa); thus, choices A and C are described in the passage. However, the passage specifies that only the royal family had access to the *harem,* which is defined as "private area," so choice B does not match the passage. The correct answer is D.

QUESTIONS

Q–205

Unparalleled, as used in this passage, means

(A) common.

(B) shabby.

(C) unequaled.

(D) sumptuous.

Your Answer _____

_____

ANSWERS

A–205

(C) <u>Unparalleled</u> means "without equal." Of the choices listed, *unequaled* is closest in meaning (choice C). *Sumptuous* is a descriptor of luxury, but it is not a synonym for <u>unparalleled</u>; *common* is a near opposite of <u>unparalleled</u>, and *shabby* is the opposite of "unparalleled luxury." The correct answer is C.

QUESTIONS

Rome in the 18th century was the art capital of the world. Because it was a papal state at that time, it was bolstered by the patronage of the popes and became a destination for cultivated people from all over the world. New styles and techniques were nurtured and developed with wide encouragement, and artists of all media flocked there. The French painters Ingres and David viewed the masterpieces on display, as did American painters, such as Copley and West. The grandeur that these and many other artists beheld in Rome was echoed in their works.

Q–206

The main idea of this passage is:

(A) Because Rome was the center of the art world at that time, it profoundly influenced the artists of the 18th century.

(B) Only Italian artists visited Rome in the 18th century; artists in France and the United States stayed in their own countries.

(C) The popes of the 18th century did not encourage or support artists of the time.

(D) Artists who visited Rome during the 18th century did not reflect what they saw there in their own works.

Your Answer _____

_____

ANSWERS

A-206

(A)   The main idea of the passage is that because Rome was the center of the art world at that time, it profoundly influenced the artists of the 18th century (choice A). The passage clearly contradicts all the other statements: It specifies that artists flocked to Rome, that the popes of the time encouraged artists and developed their talents, and that the artists who visited Rome reflected its "grandeur" in their works. The correct answer is A. (If you are unsure of the meaning of *grandeur*, "grand" is a contextual clue.)

QUESTIONS

Upon her death in 1973, Marjorie Merriweather Post bequeathed her Hillwood Estate in Washington, D.C., to the public. Hillwood Museum and Gardens features a comprehensive collection of 18th- and 19th-century Russian imperial art and the crown worn by Tsarina Alexandra at her marriage to Tsar Nicholas II in 1884. The museum also boasts a large collection of 18th-century French artistic objects, in particular, many pieces of Sèvres porcelain. The 26-acre estate includes a formal French garden, a circular rose garden, and a Japanese-style garden with waterfall.

Q–207

As described in this passage:

(A) The Hillwood Museum and Gardens showcases only European styles.

(B) Russian royalty did not wear crowns.

(C) The Hillwood features many Russian objects, but no French porcelain.

(D) The Hillwood offers an impressive amount of European objects, as well as European and Asian gardens.

Your Answer _____

_____

ANSWERS

A–207

(D) The passage describes the Hillwood Museum and Gardens as having Russian imperial art, French Sèvres porcelain, and French and Japanese gardens. It also states that the collection includes the crown worn by Russian Tsarina Alexandra. Choices A, B, and C do not match the passage's description. The correct answer is D.

QUESTIONS

Colds and flu can sneak up on you in any season. We've stopped blaming flying venom and the evil eye for causing them but still have not found a cure for either one. The viruses that cause colds and flu come in hundreds of different forms, which, over time, have adapted by changing their sizes and shapes and then lingering in, or returning to, households to infect others. Both the common cold and the flu are short-lived infections that affect the upper respiratory tract. The flu makes you feel feverish and achy, and full recovery from it can take as long as 2 weeks. Common colds usually cause a stuffy or runny nose, sneezing, and a sore throat and usually run their course in about a week.

Q–208

The author of this passage would probably agree that:

(A) Colds and flu are caused by the same virus, but colds are more serious.

(B) Colds and flu are caused by bacteria and are equally awful to combat.

(C) Colds attack the upper respiratory tract, but flu is a digestive disorder.

(D) Both colds and flu are caused by viruses, but flu has more severe symptoms and takes longer to recover from.

Your Answer _____

_____

ANSWERS

A–208

(D) The author of this passage would probably agree that both colds and flu are caused by viruses, but flu has more severe symptoms and takes longer to recover from (choice D). The passage specifies that both are caused by viruses; the plural form indicates that the same virus does not cause both illnesses. Flu is clearly described as more serious (contextual clue: "aches and fever") and takes longer to recover from (up to 2 weeks for flu, but only about a week for colds). No mention is made of bacteria, and both are described as affecting the upper respiratory tract—do not let terms like "stomach flu" fool you into thinking that flu is a digestive disorder. The correct answer is D.

QUESTIONS

In Mexico, almost 25 million people (almost one-quarter of Mexico's population) work in agriculture. In comparison, only 3 to 5 percent of the population of Europe works in agriculture. In the United States, this number is less than 2 percent. To help save the Mexican people's livelihood, traditions, and land, a special project to encourage small-scale farmers to continue to cultivate the land (rather than migrate to cities) in order to earn a living is being tested. Certain Mexican economists have stated that the farmers of Mexico were "the big losers" in the 1994 North American Free Trade Agreement (NAFTA). Nevertheless, the farmers of southern Mexico have been successful in their efforts to grow organic sesame seeds, a cash crop that does not appear to be affected by NAFTA.

Q–209

This passage indicates that:

(A) Mexican economists do not consider sesame a key crop.

(B) Sesame farmers in southern Mexico are moderately successful, despite NAFTA.

(C) Only large farms exist in Mexico at this time.

(D) Mexican farmers have immigrated to cities in Europe.

Your Answer _____

_____

ANSWERS

A–209

(B)   This passage indicates that certain Mexican economists believe small farmers were hurt by NAFTA; however, farmers in southern Mexico are succeeding with cash crops of organic sesame seed. In addition, there is a special project that encourages small-scale farmers to remain in agriculture, rather than migrate to cities. Choices A, C, and D do not match the passage. The correct answer is B.

QUESTIONS

Use the following passage to answer questions 210 and 211.

If you live on the East Coast of the United States, one of the hardiest palms to grow is the Jelly Palm (*Butia capitata*), which thrives as far north as Washington, D.C. Native to South America (from southern Brazil to Argentina), this palm reaches a height of 15 to 20 feet and has a thick trunk covered with old frond bases until it is several years old. The fronds are feather-shaped, bluish gray-green in color, and arch upward and outward, recurving so much that they sometimes touch the trunk and/or the ground. The tree produces fruit that is round or oval, orange or reddish in color (approximately 1 to 1½ inches in size). The fibrous, juicy fruit is not produced until the palm is 3 to 5 years old, but is worth waiting for! The eponymous and excellent-tasting jelly made from this fruit gives the tree its name.

Q–210

The author of this passage probably

(A)   does not know much about plants or gardening.

(B)   would recommend planting a Jelly Palm in South Florida.

(C)   would tell gardening enthusiasts that their Jelly Palms will yield fruit the first summer after they are planted.

(D)   does not find the fronds of Jelly Palms interesting.

Your Answer _____

ANSWERS

A–210

(B) The passage specifies that the Jelly Palm thrives on the U.S. East Coast, as far north as Washington, D.C., so the author would recommend planting one in South Florida (choice B). Given the topic of the passage, it is not likely that the author does not know much about plants or gardening (ruling out choice A). The passage specifies that the Jelly Palm does not yield fruit for the first 3 to 5 years, ruling out choice C. An entire sentence is devoted to describing the fronds of the Jelly Palm, so the author must find them interesting, ruling out choice D. The correct answer is B.

QUESTIONS

Q–211

Eponymous, as used in this passage, means

(A) jelly-like.

(B) fruity.

(C) good-tasting.

(D) giving its name to.

Your Answer _____

_____

ANSWERS

A–211

(D) *Eponymous* means "giving a name to something" (choice D). Contextually, the clues are the *and* between "eponymous" and "excellent-tasting," as well as "gives the tree its name," all of which should help you rule out the other choices. The correct answer is D.

QUESTIONS

For millennia, jade has been revered throughout Asia as the most precious of all stones, one that ensures good luck and good health and banishes evil spirits. The word *jade* refers to two distinctly different stones, nephrite and jadeite, which have similar properties. Nephrite, the jade carved in China for thousands of years, is a calcium magnesium silicate with hardness of 6 to 6.5 on the Mohs scale (slightly softer than quartz). Translucent to opaque, nephrite's subtle colors include creamy white, celadon, spinach, russet, and yellow. Jadeite is a sodium aluminum silicate, slightly harder and a bit less tough than nephrite. Its colors are more vivid and include green, white, russet, black, and lavender.

Q–212

The main idea of this passage is:

(A) Nephrite jade has healing properties; jadeite does not.

(B) Asians revere the benefits of all types of jade, but prefer the colors of jadeite.

(C) Asians revere the benefits of all types of jade; nephrite and jadeite are both beautiful, depending upon one's own color preferences.

(D) The colors of jade don't matter—it is more valuable than the rarest diamond.

Your Answer _____

_____

ANSWERS

A–212

(C) The purpose of this passage is to explain that Asians revere the benefits of all types of jade (context clues: "good health," "good luck," and "prosperity," plus "banish evil spirits"), and that nephrite and jadeite are both beautiful but their color ranges are different (choice C). The passage states that all jade has healing properties (ruling out choice A) and that Asians have long revered jade, but it in no way indicates any color preference or comparison of jade to diamonds (ruling out choices B and D). The correct answer is C.

QUESTIONS

Steel-frame houses are extremely energy efficient and are an ideal project for the do-it-yourself builder. The steel members are predrilled and marked, so they bolt together like a huge erector set. These houses have been shown to withstand 170-mph hurricane winds and have a seismic zone 4 earthquake rating. They are also not hospitable to termite colonies. The cost of having a steel-frame house built is typically less than a wood-frame house and even lower if you and your friends do some of the work. When completed, the house looks just like any wood-frame or masonry house.

Q–213

The author of this passage would agree that:

(A) Steel-frame houses are an excellent choice for everyone, especially those living in areas susceptible to hurricanes and earthquakes.

(B) Do-it-yourselfers need professional guidance in order to build a steel-frame house.

(C) Steel-frame houses are cost-effective and safe, but they are not as attractive as wood-frame or masonry homes.

(D) Termites thrive in steel-frame houses.

Your Answer _____

_____

ANSWERS

A–213

(A) The author of this passage would agree that steel-frame houses are an excellent choice for everyone, especially those living in areas susceptible to hurricanes and earthquakes. The passage states that do-it-yourselfers *do not* need professional guidance in order to build a steel-frame house (ruling out choice B). Further, it states that steel-frame houses are cost-effective and safe and look just like wood-frame or masonry houses (ruling out choice C); in addition, it says that they are not hospitable to termite colonies, which means termites could not thrive in them (ruling out choice D). The correct answer is A.

QUESTIONS

Although the inscription on its pediment says that Agrippa, son of Lucius, built the Pantheon, it was actually built by Emperor Hadrian (circa A.D. 125) at the middle of a bend in the Tiber River that cradles the historic center of Rome. The Pantheon is what is architecturally termed a "perfect space" because the diameter of its rotunda (dome) is 142 feet—exactly the same as its height. The most spectacular feature of the Pantheon is its oculus: a 29-foot-wide opening in the center of the dome, which serves as an inside-out sundial. The shaft of light that shines through it slowly moves across the dome during the course of the day, allowing a well-trained eye to tell the time by it. The Pantheon has a deep connection to nature through the elements of light and sky; in bad weather, the rain pours through the oculus and collects in a drain at the center of the floor.

Q–214

The passage explains that:

(A) The Pantheon bears the name of Agrippa but was actually built by Emperor Hadrian.

(B) The Pantheon's oculus acts as a sundial but does not let it rain into the interior space.

(C) The Pantheon is a "perfect space" and the oculus in its dome is its most outstanding feature.

(D) A and C, but not B.

Your Answer _____

_____

ANSWERS

A–214

(D)   The passage explains that the Pantheon bears the name of Agrippa but was actually built by Emperor Hadrian; it also describes the Pantheon as a "perfect space," with the oculus in its dome being its most outstanding feature. However, it is explained that the Pantheon's oculus, although it does function as a sundial, as an open-air hole, also allows rain into the interior space, where it collects in a drain at the center of the floor. Choices A and C match the passage, but choice B does not. The correct answer is D.

QUESTIONS

Most people have favorite colors and know when certain colors look "right" together. They can also tell when a color combination falls flat. As most first-year design students learn, there is a science to color matching. The key is to understand the color wheel, whose 12 segments consist of primary, secondary, and tertiary hues, along with their tints and shades. The three primary colors are red, blue, and yellow. As all other colors are combinations of two or three primaries, every hue consists of varying proportions of red, blue, or yellow. To appear balanced, a color scheme should consist of hues that, taken together, contain equal amounts of the three primary colors. The color wheel helps to recognize and calculate these relationships.

Q–215

From the passage we can infer that:

(A) Choosing colors is purely artistic and has nothing to do with math or science.

(B) Color matching involves the use of color balance and color combination.

(C) The 12-segmented color wheel consists of hues, tints, and shades.

(D) B and C, but not A.

Your Answer _____

_____

ANSWERS

A–215

(D) From this passage we can infer that color matching involves the use of color balance and color combination (this is stated in the passage) and the 12-segmented color wheel consists of hues, tints, and shades (this is also stated in the passage). But nothing in the passage would indicate that science and math are not involved in color matching—in fact, the passage specifies that there is a science to color matching and that the color wheel helps to recognize and calculate these relationships (the contextual clue that math is involved is the word *calculate*). Choices B and C are supported by the passage, but choice A is not. The correct answer is D.

QUESTIONS

Dahlias bring tropical energy wherever they are planted. With blooms that can be as simple as a daisy or as exotic as a giant cactus flower, dahlias grow from underground tubers that resemble sweet potatoes. When Spanish explorers found them in Mexico, they were grown as a food crop. People did not begin to grow them for their flowers until about 200 years ago. There were 6 varieties at that time—as compared with about 20,000 today. Dahlias come in 18 very different flower types, with such names as anemone, cactus, orchid pompon, and waterlily.

Q–216

According to the passage, dahlias

(A)   are tropical but do not always look exotic.

(B)   are a delicacy in Mexico, where they are not grown as flowers.

(C)   look like daisies and do not come in many varieties.

(D)   are different from the anemone and the orchid pompon.

Your Answer _____

_____

ANSWERS

A–216

(A) According to the passage, dahlias are tropical but do not always look exotic (the passage specifies this). The passage also states that dahlias were grown as a food crop in Mexico during the days of the Spanish conquest but have been grown for their flowers for the past 200 years (ruling out choice B); may be like daisies and now come in 20,000 varieties (ruling out choice C); include flower types called "anemone" and "orchid pompon" (ruling out choice D). The correct answer is A.

QUESTIONS

From the 1830s to the 1920s, more than 50 showboats carried stage shows and circuses to river towns throughout America's heartland. The showboat was generally a large scow-form barge pushed by a separate towboat. The *Majestic,* built in 1923 by Tom J. Reynolds to replace an earlier version with the same name, usually presented one show per stop and then moved on. In the 1990s, the City of Cincinnati owned the *Majestic,* which was moored on the banks of the Ohio River near Central Bridge in downtown Cincinnati.

Q–217

A good title for this passage might be:

(A) The *Majestic*: The Story of a River Showboat.

(B) Cincinnati Song and Dance.

(C) Showboats Still Sailing in the Midwest.

(D) The Life and Times of Tom J. Reynolds.

Your Answer _____

_____

ANSWERS

QUESTIONS

Use the following passage to answer questions 218 and 219.

American director Peter Sellers' idea of basing an opera on recent world events resulted in his collaboration with composer John Adams, American poet Alice Goodman (as librettist), and choreographer Mark Morris. This team created two operas: *Nixon in China,* based on the 1972 Beijing meeting between U.S. President Richard Nixon and Chairman Mao Zedong of the People's Republic of China; and *The Death of Klinghoffer,* which reenacted the infamous 1985 hijacking of the luxury liner *Achille Lauro* by Palestinian terrorists, who subsequently murdered Leon Klinghoffer, a paralyzed American tourist on vacation with his wife. The first opera premiered in 1987 at the Brown Theater in Houston, Texas; the second, in 1991 at the Theatre de la Monnaie in Brussels and the Brooklyn Academy of Music in New York. Both works received critical acclaim for their iconoclastic artistry.

Q–218

The author of this passage believes that:

(A) Contemporary events can be effectively utilized for dramatic interpretation in operatic work.

(B) Sellers found it difficult to find collaborators because his ideas were not mainstream.

(C) The performances were financially successful but received poor reviews.

(D) None of the above.

Your Answer _____

ANSWERS

A–218

(A) It can be deduced from the complimentary tone of the passage that the author believes that contemporary events can be effectively utilized for dramatic interpretation in operatic work (choice A). The passage does not indicate that Sellers found it difficult to find collaborators because his ideas were not mainstream; nor does it indicate that the performances were financially successful, but specifies that the works received critical acclaim (that is, good reviews)—which rules out choices B and C, respectively. Always be cautious about answer choices of "none of the above," especially in paragraph comprehension questions. The correct answer is A.

QUESTIONS

Q–219

<u>Iconoclastic</u>, as used in this passage, means

(A) artistic.

(B) computerized.

(C) nonconformist.

(D) musical.

Your Answer _____

ANSWERS

A–219

(C) <u>Iconoclastic</u> means "attacking or cynically viewing popular institutions and beliefs and/or public figures"; closest to it in meaning from among the choices listed is *nonconformist* (choice C). The sentence uses the word *artistry*, so *artistic* would be redundant; *computerized* and *musical* are in no way related. The correct answer is C. (Do not be fooled by "icon-" as being in any way related to computer icons; *icon* means "image," and another synonym for <u>iconoclastic</u> is *image-shattering*.)

QUESTIONS

The 1893 World's Columbian Exposition in Chicago—dedicated in 1892 to coincide with the 400th anniversary of the arrival of Columbus in the New World—was meant to prove America's coming of age. At the time, Americans thought of themselves as the final step in 3,000 years of evolution, and they wanted the Chicago fair to demonstrate America's cultural and technical superiority. Built in record time, the fair covered 686 acres of landscaped parkland, with gigantic Beaux Arts-style creamy-white exhibition halls and 60 acres of waterways and "Venetian lagoons." Some 27 million people visited what came to be called the Chicago World's Fair. The fair published a newsletter in 14 languages and presented the world with the first Ferris wheel.

Q–220

According to this passage, the World's Columbian Exposition in Chicago:

(A) Began in Venice, but was later moved to Chicago to celebrate the voyage of Columbus.

(B) The Beaux Arts style emphasizes dark-colored buildings.

(C) Millions of people attended the fair, and one of its best-known firsts is the Ferris wheel.

(D) The World's Columbian Exposition in Chicago is different from the Chicago World's Fair, but the two are often confused.

Your Answer _____

_____

ANSWERS

A–220

(C) According to this passage, 27 million people attended the World's Columbian Exposition in Chicago, where the first Ferris wheel was presented. Although the fair featured "Venetian lagoons" as part of its landscape, the fair was located in Chicago and was never in Venice (ruling out choice A). The passage describes "Beaux Arts-style creamy-white exhibition halls" (ruling out choice B). The passage states that the World's Columbian Exposition in Chicago was later called the Chicago World's Fair (ruling out choice D). The correct answer is C.

QUESTIONS

The first recorded discovery of tourmalines in the United States was in Maine in 1822. The Maine deposits tend to produce crystals in raspberry pink-red, as well as minty greens. California became a large producer in the early 1900s, and its deposits are known for bright pinks and interesting bicolors. Maine and California were the world's largest producers of gem tourmalines during the early 1900s. The Empress Dowager of China loved pink tourmaline, as a gemstone for both jewelry and decorative carvings, and she bought large quantities of the stone from a mine in San Diego, California. Native Americans have used pink and green tourmalines as funeral gifts for centuries.

Q–221

From this passage we can infer that:

(A) Tourmaline comes in many colors, except pink and green.

(B) California mines did not produce pink tourmaline.

(C) Some Native American tribes buried their dead with tourmaline amulets.

(D) In the early part of the 20th century, most of the world's tourmalines came from Maine and California.

Your Answer _____

_____

ANSWERS

A-221

(D) From this passage we can infer that in the early part of the 20th century, most of the world's tourmalines came from Maine and California (choice D); the passage specifically mentions that these two states were the world's largest producers of tourmaline in the early 1900s. The passage also describes pink and green tourmaline specifically and describes the Empress Dowager of China as having obtained large quantities of pink tourmaline from a mine in San Diego (ruling out choices A and B, respectively). The last sentence explains that Native Americans traditionally give pink and green tourmalines as funeral gifts, but it does not specify that these stones are buried with the dead (ruling out choice C). The correct answer is D.

QUESTIONS

The French sculptor Antoine-Louis Bayre was born into poverty in 1795, had little formal schooling, and almost never left Paris—so his choice of subjects for his art is very surprising. For more than 50 years, he created bronze sculptures of lions, tigers, reptiles, and birds of prey in what could be called photographic detail. He often showed these creatures in mortal combat, at the moment just before the kill. His representations of this raw violence have fascinated people worldwide for almost 200 years. Bayre's sculptures are on display in such museums as the Louvre and the Musée d'Orsay in Paris, the National Gallery of Art in Washington, D.C., and the J. Paul Getty Museum in Los Angeles.

Q–222

The author of this passage would probably agree that:

(A) The best artists have witnessed firsthand whatever subjects they depict.

(B) Although moderately popular, Bayre has never had exhibits outside of France.

(C) Bayre's sculptures are known for their realistic, visceral quality.

(D) Fans of Bayre's work find it appealing because of its representation of peaceful animals at rest and play.

Your Answer _____

_____

ANSWERS

A–222

(C) The author of this passage would probably agree that Bayre's sculptures are known for their realistic, visceral quality (choice C); contextual clues include "photographic detail" (*realistic*) and "raw violence" (*visceral*). The author would not agree that the best artists have witnessed firsthand whatever subjects they depict (ruling out choice A).

The passage lists two museums in the United States where Bayre's works are on display, and it specifies that people are fascinated by the raw violence in his animal sculptures (ruling out choices B and D, respectively). The correct answer is C.

QUESTIONS

Over the centuries, plants have revealed their medicinal properties to people in many ways—from the Native Americans who found the perfect blood purifier in the red blooms of the burdock plant to the North Africans who found relief from the pain of damp-induced rheumatism in the wet-loving willow tree. In modern times, doctors practicing alternative medicine believe that warming herbs relieve chronic problems characterized as deficiencies. Tonic herbs build your body back up, and cooling herbs remove heat in acute situations that are characterized by excess.

Q–223

This passage supports which statement(s)?

(A) Plants have a great amount of healing properties, and contemporary alternative medicine practitioners use them to treat chronic conditions.

(B) Native Americans used the willow tree as a blood purifier.

(C) Tonic herbs rebuild the immune system; cooling herbs, which remove heat, are used in extremely serious circumstances.

(D) A and C, but not B.

Your Answer _____

_____

ANSWERS

A–223

(D) According to this passage, plants have a great amount of healing properties, and contemporary alternative medicine practitioners use them to treat chronic conditions. In addition, tonic herbs rebuild the immune system; cooling herbs, which remove heat, are used in extremely serious circumstances. However, Native Americans used the burdock plant, not the willow tree, as a blood purifier. Choices A and C match the passage, but choice B does not. The correct answer is D.

QUESTIONS

Use the following passage to answer questions 224 and 225.

Researchers now view glaucoma as a disease of the brain—that is, a neurodegenerative disease, rather than simply an ophthalmological disease. Recent research has shown that the complex connection between the eye and the brain is an important key to the disease. Glaucoma shares a number of similarities with degenerative brain diseases, such as Alzheimer's, Parkinson's, and Lou Gehrig's disease. In all these diseases, age and family history are significant risk factors and specific areas of the brain are damaged over time. The only difference between them and glaucoma is that the specific area of the brain affected by glaucoma is the one related to the eye and the optic nerve.

Q–224

The main idea of this passage is:

(A) Degenerative brain diseases must be studied further in order to treat glaucoma.

(B) Glaucoma, because of its similarities with degenerative brain diseases, is now being studied as a neurodegenerative disease.

(C) Degenerative brain diseases, which rapidly destroy the entire brain, must be studied in conjunction with glaucoma, which impacts the eye in a similar fashion.

(D) Glaucoma is an important disease to study because of its effect on the eye, but it does not impact the brain.

Your Answer _____

ANSWERS

A–224

(B) The main idea of this passage is that glaucoma is now being studied as a neurodegenerative disease because of its similarities with other such diseases (choice B). The statement in no ways indicates that degenerative brain diseases must be studied further in order to treat glaucoma (ruling out choice A). Degenerative brain diseases are described as impacting specific parts of the brain over time, as glaucoma does with the eye (ruling out choice C). The whole point of the passage is that glaucoma, traditionally thought of as an eye disease, needs to be studied further because there is a complex connection between the eye and the brain, and new research shows that glaucoma influences this connection (ruling out choice D). The correct answer is B.

QUESTIONS

Q–225

Ophthalmological, as used in this passage, means

(A) genetic.

(B) eye-related.

(C) age-related.

(D) medically researched.

Your Answer _____

_____

ANSWERS

A–225

(B) *Ophthalmological* means "of or related to the eye" (choice B). Although the passage refers to medical research and describes degenerative brain diseases as being related to heredity and age, the other choices are not related in meaning to *ophthalmological*. The contextual clues are the passage's constant reference to glaucoma as a disease of the eye. The correct answer is B.

QUESTIONS

Tower Grove Park, located in the south-central section of St. Louis, Missouri, is said to be the nation's best-preserved 19th-century Gardenesque-style park. Modeled after a form popular in England and France that featured winding paths lined with native and exotic plants, the park boasts 285 acres containing 8,000 trees of 100 different species and is highlighted by numerous ornate pavilions, gateways, and statues. Tower Grove was originally the home of Henry Shaw, a wealthy St. Louis hardware merchant who wanted to create a botanical garden patterned after those he had seen in Europe. He later donated the property to the city, which opened it as a public park in 1872.

Q–226

The passage supports which statement(s)?

(A) Tower Grove was a private estate prior to its owner's donating it to the city of St. Louis to be a public park.

(B) Henry Shaw commissioned Tower Grove to resemble the gardens of Europe.

(C) Tower Grove Park is filled with all types of plants and trees but has no man-made structures.

(D) A and B, but not C.

Your Answer _____

_____

ANSWERS

(D)   According to the passage, Tower Grove was a private estate prior to its owner, Henry Shaw, donating it to the city of St. Louis to be a public park. Shaw commissioned Tower Grove because he wanted gardens that resembled the gardens of Europe. However, the passage also specifies that Tower Grove Park is filled with thousands of native and exotic plants and trees, as well as various pavilions, gateways, and statues. Choices A and B match the passage, but choice C does not. The correct answer is D.

QUESTIONS

The talented artisans of ancient China were as valued by their society as computer-technology experts are valued in ours today. Over the millennia, especially during the Warring States period, wherever there was a conflict, all the captives were killed except for the artisans. Skilled workmen were considered more valuable than farmers, cattle, or horses. After a battle, the conquerors took the time to sort out the captives. The artisans knew they and their families would be saved. Weavers, jade cutters, bronze workers, and wood carvers were rounded up and shipped off to the state of the conqueror.

Q–227

The main idea of this passage is:

(A) In ancient China, craftsmen were respected by all and spared during wars.

(B) During the Warring States period, the artisans in ancient China outsmarted their captors and avoided capture.

(C) Ancient Chinese conquerors were merciless toward all their captives, especially the artisans.

(D) Weavers and jade cutters were respected, but bronze workers and wood carvers were captured and sent away.

Your Answer _____

ANSWERS

A–227

(A) The main idea of this passage is that ancient Chinese craftsmen were respected by all and spared during times of war and conflict (choice A). The passage specifies that these artisans' lives were spared because they were valued but that they were taken by their captors (ruling out choices B and C). The passage also specifies that all types of artisans, because of their value, were sorted out and shipped off to the home of the conqueror (ruling out choice D). The correct answer is A.

QUESTIONS

When one thinks of Celtic heroes, the legendary Arthur is the name that immediately comes to mind. He was most popular during the Middle Ages when the adventures of his followers, the Knights of the Round Table, impressed most of Western Europe. Arthur was the son of the British king Uther Pendragon and Igraine, wife of the Cornish Duke of Gorlois. Conceived out of wedlock, he was brought up far away from his parents by Merlin the wizard. Even though most of the earliest stories about Arthur are found in 7th-century Welsh poems, there is no doubt that the warlike king belongs to the heroic myths and traditions of both Wales and Ireland, as he appears in several Irish sagas as well.

Q–228

The passage supports which statement(s)?

(A) The legends of Arthur influenced Welsh poetry, but not Irish sagas.

(B) The adventures of Arthur and the Knights of the Round Table were popular during the Middle Ages in Western Europe.

(C) Merlin was an important figure in Arthurian legend.

(D) B and C, but not A.

Your Answer _____

_____

ANSWERS

A–228

(D) According to the passage, the adventures of Arthur and the Knights of the Round Table were popular during the Middle Ages in Western Europe, and Merlin, the wizard who raised Arthur, was an important figure in Arthurian legend. However, the passage specifically states that the legends of Arthur influenced both Welsh poetry and Irish sagas. Choices B and C match the passage, but choice A does not. The correct answer is D.

QUESTIONS

Turtles are reptiles that have inhabited our planet since the dinosaurs roamed the earth. They have survived because they are tough, adaptable, and the result of a long evolutionary process, which included flexible behavior patterns and a unique body design. Whether they can survive in today's world, as their environments are disrupted or destroyed, depends more on the actions of human beings than on the turtles themselves. Many cultures have a great heritage of tales and folklore regarding these amazing creatures. Ancient Hindu, Chinese, Japanese, Mayan, and Native American myths give both praise and respect to turtles. We could do well to learn from these cultures!

Q–229

The author of this passage would probably defend which of the following statements?

(A) Turtle habitats do not need to be preserved because they have survived a long time and know how to adapt to any environment.

(B) The civilizations that revered the turtle did not know very much.

(C) Turtles are amazing creatures that have a long history and deserve respect and protection from humans.

(D) Scientists cannot figure out the mystery of turtles' survival; certainly it is not because of their shells.

Your Answer _____

_____

ANSWERS

QUESTIONS

Many of the problems with putting strokes can be linked to an incorrect length of the stroke. In a proper pendulum putting stroke, the take-away and the follow-through should be the same distance. There should also be a consistent rhythm to both. This rhythm should be the same for a 5-foot putt and a 50-foot putt. The only adjustment for a longer putt should be both a longer take-away and a longer follow-through. To develop the feel of a correct pendulum stroke you should practice with a long putter. Set up a practice drill of three targets at distances ranging from about 20 to 60 feet. After hitting all putts with a long putter, repeat the drill with a regular putter. The length of stroke and rhythm should be the same as with the long putter. This drill will help you develop a more consistent putting stroke that will lead to lower scores on the golf course.

Q–230

The main idea of this passage is:

(A) If you work on the length and rhythm of your stroke, you will improve your putt.

(B) The stroke length and rhythm are not tied to better putting.

(C) Lower your scores on the golf course.

(D) Do not practice take-away or follow-through; just do practice drills.

Your Answer _____

_____

ANSWERS

A–230

(A) The main idea of the passage is that if you work on the length and rhythm of your stroke, you will improve your putt (choice A), and the passage describes how to accomplish this. The stroke length and rhythm are tied to better putting, and working on take-away and follow-through, as well as practice drills, all are recommended in the passage. The main idea of the passage cannot be a statement that contradicts what the passage states (ruling out choices B and D). Although the passage ends with the statement that improving your putt will lower your scores on the golf course, this is not the main idea, just a word of encouragement to the beginning golfer (ruling out choice C). The correct answer is A. (Remember that the main idea is one that carries through the entire passage; a main-idea identification must reflect more than just one sentence in the passage, even if it accurately reflects that sentence, as described above as the reason to rule out choice C.)

QUESTIONS

Among the fall harvest, the pear is enjoyed as much as the apple. Unlike most tree fruits, pears are best ripened off the tree so that they can ripen evenly and smoothly for a creamy texture. When allowed to ripen on the tree, they develop stones (grit cells) in their flesh, a process that cannot take place if ripened off the tree. Pears are very beneficial to eat, as they have many health benefits: They aid digestion by cleaning the entire digestive system; their iodine content helps the thyroid gland to function well, keeping the body's metabolism in good balance. In addition, pears are virtually fat-free, low in calories, and promote smooth skin and shiny hair.

Q–231

According to the passage:

(A) Pears are an extremely popular summer fruit.

(B) Pears are extremely healthful and are beneficial to the digestive and metabolic systems, as well as skin and hair.

(C) Pears are high in fat and calories, but their nutritional value outweighs those drawbacks if they are eaten in moderation.

(D) Only buy tree-ripened pears to avoid fruit with a gritty texture.

Your Answer _____

ANSWERS

A–231

(B)   According to the passage, pears are extremely healthful and are beneficial to the digestive and metabolic systems, as well as skin and hair (choice B). The passage specifies that pears are an extremely popular fall-harvest fruit, low in fat and calories (ruling out choices A and C). The passage also explains in detail that pears should be ripened off the tree in order to avoid fruit with a gritty texture (ruling out choice D). The correct answer is B.

QUESTIONS

Use the following passage to answer questions 232 and 233.

Temperance advocates, who cheered the passage of the Volstead Act (the law that initiated Prohibition) and the demise of the saloon, had no idea how speakeasies would be created or how many Americans would produce alcohol at home. For the cost of 6 or 7 dollars, anyone could purchase a portable still at most hardware stores. In addition, an inexperienced person could go to the local library and find thousands of explanations—in books, magazine articles, and even government pamphlets—that described in detail the steps for distilling alcohol by using raw materials like prunes, apples, bananas, watermelon, potato peelings, oats, or barley. Those who didn't want to smell up their kitchens could purchase a legally produced California product called Vine-Glo—a grape juice which, when put in the cellar to sit for 60 days, turned into a wine that was 15 percent alcohol. California wine growers thrived during Prohibition, expanding their land use from 97,000 acres in 1919 to 681,000 acres in 1926.

Q–232

From the passage, it can be deduced that Prohibition

(A)   might have made the preparation and consumption of alcohol illegal, but it did not stop people from manufacturing or drinking alcohol.

(B)   was the reason why many people used everyday items to inexpensively produce their own alcohol at home.

(C)   spurred the growth of the California wine industry.

(D)   All of the above.

Your Answer _____

_____

ANSWERS

A–232

(D) From the passage it can be deduced that Prohibition might have made the preparation and consumption of alcohol illegal, but it did not stop people from manufacturing or drinking alcohol; was the reason why many people used everyday items to inexpensively produce their own alcohol at home; and spurred the growth of the California wine industry. All the choices contain information that *can be deduced from the passage,* so the correct answer is D. Read the question carefully! When a question specifies the information *can be deduced* from the passage, it means that you will have to look harder and draw more conclusions.

QUESTIONS

Q–233

Temperance, as used in this passage, means

(A) anger.

(B) calm.

(C) abstinence.

(D) personality.

Your Answer _____

ANSWERS

A–233

(C) <u>Temperance</u> means "restraint" but is frequently used to connote *abstinence* from alcohol (it was used extensively in this sense prior to and during Prohibition). Even if you do not remember your U.S. history from World War I through the Great Depression and so don't recall hearing of the temperance movement, you can determine that the other choices all are inaccurate synonyms for temperance: *anger* could be a good choice for a word close in meaning to *temper*; *calm* could be a good choice for a word close in meaning to *tempest*; *personality* could be a good choice for a word close in meaning to *temperament*. The correct answer is C. (If all else fails, use other contextual clues: If *temperance* advocates cheered Prohibition and disapproved of alcohol, the only thing among the choices listed that they would approve of is *abstinence*—neither anger nor calm nor personality would fit as accurate choices, ruling them all out.)

QUESTIONS

The Internet was not invented by a single person, but if you chose to say that any single individual began the most important basic thinking about what would have to go into a system whereby machines talked to each other, credit should be given to American mathematician, physiologist, and engineering genius Norbert Wiener, who first thought about talking machines during the course of World War II. Wiener worked to develop a system by which one machine—the radar device that would locate an enemy airplane and calculate its course—would communicate with another machine—the anti-aircraft gun, "telling it" where to aim to hit the target. It may seem like no big deal to us now, but at the time, it was big stuff for Wiener, who had the insight to understand where the technology might lead. He said, "It is the purpose of cybernetics (from a Greek word that means "to steer or govern") to develop a language and techniques that will enable us indeed to attack the problem of control and communication." Norbert Wiener died in 1964. It would be interesting to hear the comments he would have made regarding today's use of the Internet.

Q–234

The author of the passage would most likely agree that:

(A) Norbert Wiener's engineering genius not only helped the Allies win World War II, it also paved the way for today's technological advances.

(B) Inventors of technology might have a vision of the future forms that technology will take, but only time can prove or disprove it.

(C) Cybernetics is the study of governmental control.

(D) A and B, but not C.

Your Answer _____

ANSWERS

A–234

(D) The author of the passage would most likely agree that Norbert Wiener's engineering genius not only helped the Allies win World War II, it also paved the way for today's technological advances, and that inventors of technology might have a vision of the future forms that technology will take, but only time can prove or disprove it. Both statements can be determined from the author's praise of Wiener as an engineering genius who developed certain key technology during World War II (as the Allies won the war, the American Wiener's developments had to have assisted their victory), as well as the citation of Wiener's views on technology and the author's closing comment that it would be interesting to know what Wiener would have thought of contemporary use of the Internet. However, cybernetics is not described as the study of governmental control. Thus, choices A and B correspond to the passage, but choice C does not. The correct answer is D.

QUESTIONS

Sericulture, the cultivation of the domestic silkworm, is an enormously complex and painstaking process that requires expert handling of the eggs, caterpillars, and cocoons. For thousands of years, the Chinese kept secret the knowledge of how silk was made. Early in the 20th century, however, the pioneering Swedish textile scholar Vivi Sylwan published a report of archaeological findings from the Shang period tombs north of the Yellow River. These findings, which included a fossilized silk cocoon and fragments of plain weave with geometrical patterns in warp floats that had been impregnated in the patina of Shang bronze vessels, indicated that both sericulture and silk weaving were well established in China more than a thousand years before the birth of Christ.

Q-235

The passage supports which statement(s)?

(A) It is a complicated and difficult procedure to cultivate silkworms for silk making.

(B) Sericulture and silk weaving existed in China during the Shang period, more than 3,000 years ago.

(C) The ancient Chinese kept sericulture a secret from everyone but the Swedish, whom they taught how to make silk.

(D) A and B, but not C.

Your Answer _____

ANSWERS

A–235

(D) According to the passage, it is a complicated and difficult procedure ("enormously complex and painstaking") to cultivate silkworms for silk making, and sericulture and silk weaving existed in China during the Shang period, more than 3,000 years ago ("more than a thousand years before Christ"). However, the passage specifies that the Chinese kept sericulture a secret from everyone; there is no indication that they taught the Swedish how to make silk—be careful not to focus on "Swedish" because of the reference to the Swedish textile scholar . . . he did not find the fossilized evidence until thousands of years later. Choices A and B are supported by the passage, but choice C is not, so the correct answer is D.

QUESTIONS

Amethyst was used as a gemstone by the ancient Egyptians and also in European antiquity for intaglios (ornamental engravings). Beads of amethyst are found in Anglo-Saxon graves in England. Although it can be found in many areas of the world, the fine, clear specimens that are suitable for cutting and polishing for use as ornamental stones are found in a comparatively few locations. Such crystals occur either in the cavities of mineral veins, in granitic rock formations, or as a lining in agate geodes. Many of the hollow agates from Brazil and Uruguay contain crops of amethyst crystals in their interiors. Much fine amethyst comes from the Ekaterinburg district of Russia, where it is found in cavities in granite rocks.

Q–236

From the passage, it can be inferred that:

(A) Amethyst used to be easy to find, but overmining has made it scarce.

(B) Amethyst is now considered a gemstone, but in ancient times it was not perceived as valuable.

(C) Amethyst is a beautiful gemstone that has been valued all over the world for thousands of years, even though it is now hard to find specimens that can be used for carving or jewelry.

(D) South American amethysts are more prized than Russian amethysts.

Your Answer _____

ANSWERS

A–236

(C) From the passage it can be inferred that amethyst is a beautiful gemstone that has been valued all over the world for thousands of years, even though it is now hard to find specimens that can be used for carving or jewelry (choice C). The passage specifies that numerous cultures in various parts of the world have used amethyst over the past few thousand years and also that "clear specimens suitable for cutting and polishing for use as ornamental stones are found in comparatively few locations." Nowhere does the passage specify that amethyst was once abundant but has since been overmined (ruling out choice A); the passage specifies amethyst's use and value in ancient times (ruling out choice B); and the passage does not indicate whether South American amethysts or Russian amethysts are more valuable (ruling out choice D). The correct answer is C. (Remember, when the question asks you to *infer from the passage,* you have to *draw conclusions* but should never select an answer choice that is not in some way supported by the passage.)

QUESTIONS

According to the American Kennel Club, the chow chows currently bred in the United States and Europe can trace their lineage back some 4,000 years to China. Even today, in some isolated mountain regions of China, Buddhist monks still raise these highly intelligent, easily trained dogs, which are prized for their hunting and guarding skills. Chow chows reached their peak of popularity in the United States during the late 1920s and early 1930s. A chow even lived in the White House—along with its owners, President and Mrs. Coolidge.

Q–237

A good title for this passage might be:

(A) Fun Facts about Chow Chows.

(B) Chow Chows in the White House.

(C) Chow Chows: Dogs for Buddhist Monks.

(D) A Brand-New Dog Breed—The Chow Chow.

Your Answer _____

_____

ANSWERS

A–237

(A) A good title for this passage might be "Fun Facts about Chow Chows" (choice A). Although choices B and C reflect information included in the passage, they would not be appropriate titles for it. The passage specifies that the chow chow has been bred for 4,000 years, so a title describing it as a brand-new breed would not be accurate (ruling out choice D). The correct answer is A.

QUESTIONS

For a thousand days, President John F. Kennedy and his wife, Jacqueline, lived in the White House and brought to it an elegance and energy so magical, the media referred to it as "Camelot." Americans could not recall a first family that had been so young, good-looking, intelligent, talented, or so brimming with vitality. Indeed, it felt like it had lasted "only one brief shining moment," when it tragically came to an end on November 22, 1963—the day that President Kennedy was assassinated in Dallas, Texas.

Q–238

The author of this passage would confirm that:

(A) The Kennedys were an intelligent, attractive and vivacious first family that captivated the media and the American people.

(B) The Kennedy administration is referred to as "Camelot" because of the first family's charm.

(C) President Kennedy is admired because he was tragically assassinated.

(D) A and B, but not C.

Your Answer _____

ANSWERS

A–238

(D) Based on the content of the passage, the author would confirm that the Kennedys were an intelligent, attractive, and vivacious first family that captivated the media and the American people, and that the Kennedy administration is referred to as "Camelot" because of the first family's charm. But, although the author describes the assassination as tragic, nothing in the passage stipulates that President Kennedy is admired because he was tragically assassinated (ruling out choice C). The author of the passage would confirm choices A and B, but not C, so the correct answer is D.

QUESTIONS

Use the following passage to answer questions 239 and 240.

The Japanese bombing of Pearl Harbor, which destroyed or crippled 18 American ships (including 8 battleships), would change the way maritime warfare was waged. The U.S. Navy soon had to face the shocking reality of one military defeat after another on the Pacific island battlefields, something never before experienced in the history of the nation. From December 7, 1941, well into 1942, the Allies were defeated on Guam, Wake Island, Hong Kong, Borneo, Singapore, the Netherlands Indies—and, most agonizing for the Americans, the surrender of the Philippines, resulting in the infamous Bataan Death March. It was not until the end of 1942 that the tide began to turn against the Japanese, when Marines and GIs leapfrogged from island to island, achieving victories on Guadalcanal, Tarawa, Eniwetok, Saipan, Ulithi, Iwo Jima, and Okinawa. In total, American forces launched more than 100 island invasions, 68 of them resulting in heavy losses. Every unit involved in the Iwo Jima invasion suffered at least a 50 percent casualty count, but Americans remained committed to victory in the Pacific, which, although hard-won, was ultimately attained.

Q–239

The main idea of the passage is:

(A) The attack on Pearl Harbor changed naval warfare, but the battles fought after it were easily won.

(B) The attack on Pearl Harbor changed naval warfare; following numerous hard-fought sea battles, the Allies eventually beat the Japanese.

(C) The attack on Pearl Harbor changed naval warfare, and that is why the Allies were defeated on Iwo Jima.

(D) The attack on Pearl Harbor changed naval warfare, and that is why the Philippines surrendered.

Your Answer _____

ANSWERS

A-239

(B) The main idea of the passage is that the attack on Pearl Harbor changed naval warfare; following numerous hard-fought sea battles, Allied troops eventually beat the Japanese (choice B). Notice that every answer choice matches the opening statement of the passage, so you can focus on the second part of each choice to determine which one is correct: The battles fought in the Pacific were not easily won (the passage describes this in detail), so you can rule out choice A; Iwo Jima is described as a victory for the Allies, so you can rule out choice C (remember to follow the passage, not information you already know, such as the famous victory of Iwo Jima); the passage does not correlate the surrender of the Philippines with the attack on Pearl Harbor, so you can rule out choice D. The correct answer is B.

QUESTIONS

Q–240

<u>Infamous</u>, as used in this passage, means

(A) notorious.

(B) cruel.

(C) not well known.

(D) painful.

Your Answer _____

ANSWERS

A–240

(A) <u>Infamous</u> means "famous for being bad or awful"; closest to it in meaning from among the choices given is *notorious* (choice A). The Bataan Death March is infamous because it was cruel and inflicted pain on the Americans and others forced to march by the Japanese, but *cruel* and *painful* are not synonyms for <u>infamous</u>; *not well known* is inaccurate, as anything infamous is well known, just not in a good way. The correct answer is A.

QUESTIONS

The deities of Greece and Rome were accompanied by many supernatural creatures—nymphs of the sea and springs (nereids and naiads), nymphs of the mountains and forests (oreads and dryads), the Three Furies, the Three Graces, the Three Fates, the Nine Muses, as well as satyrs and others. These companions acted as servants, teachers, helpers, and followers of the gods and goddesses. Each god/dess had his/her own retinue, whose characters reflected the personality of that deity. Many had other roles as spirits of specific places with special responsibilities. Some were nature spirits who must have seemed closer to the everyday life of the ancient Greeks and Romans than the mighty gods on Mount Olympus.

Q–241

According to the passage, Greek and Roman mythology:

(A) Featured supernatural creatures—nymphs, satyrs, the Muses, and others—that served and helped the gods and goddesses.

(B) Only the gods and goddesses were worshipped in ancient Greece and Rome.

(C) Because they felt closer to day-to-day circumstances, the people of those times felt closer to the nature spirits than to the mighty Olympian gods.

(D) A and C, but not B.

Your Answer _____

_____

ANSWERS

A–241

(D) According to the passage, Greek and Roman mythology featured supernatural creatures that served and helped the gods and goddesses; because they felt closer to day-to-day circumstances, the people of those times felt closer to the nature spirits than to the mighty Olympian gods. However, the passage does not indicate that only the gods and goddesses were worshipped in ancient Greece and Rome; in fact, it emphasizes that the opposite was true. Choices A and C match the passage, but choice B does not, so the correct answer is D.

QUESTIONS

By the 1940s, a number of 20th-century innovations appeared in college dormitory rooms throughout America. The portable typewriter, originally introduced in the 1930s, became more affordable, allowing students to take advantage of its lightweight design to type their course papers—often doing so on the dorm-room floor, which became their seating area of choice. The portable phonograph, introduced as early as 1921, suddenly became a "must-have." Fast-forward to the 21st century to find that the computer has become the center of the dorm room, replacing the typewriter and phonograph (and the dorm-room staple of later decades, the stereo). In the lecture hall, the laptop computer has even replaced notebooks and pens.

Q–242

The main idea of this passage is:

(A) Computers have become central components in college life.

(B) Dorm life was better in the 1940s when students used typewriters.

(C) Advances in technology do not impact college life.

(D) Computers have replaced typewriters on college campuses but will never replace stereos.

Your Answer _____

ANSWERS

A–242

(A) The main idea of this passage is that computers have become central components in college life. The passage highlights this throughout, which is what makes it the main idea. Nowhere does it state that dorm life was better in the 1940s when students used typewriters (ruling out choice B). It specifies that advances in technology impact college life and that computers have replaced typewriters and stereos on college campuses (ruling out choices C and D). The correct answer is A—remember that main-idea answer choices must reflect information that carries through the entire passage, in addition to being information supported by the passage.

QUESTIONS

On October 27, 1904, at precisely 2:00 P.M., a wall of sound shook New York City from Battery Park to Harlem. Church bells and ferry boat horns competed with the steam whistles of hundreds of power plants and the firing of salutes. Cheering citizens flocked into the streets. The first section of the New York City Subway had been completed: a 9.1-mile route from City Hall to West 145th Street. New Yorkers could now avoid the massive traffic jams and travel beneath the jammed streets. Residents of crowded urban buildings could now move to the rapidly growing "suburbs" along the ever-expanding subway route.

Q–243

From the passage, we can infer that:

(A)   The subway forever changed life in New York City.

(B)   New Yorkers were excited about the new subway, even though it shook the streets.

(C)   The first section of the subway was just a little over nine miles, but it was soon expanded.

(D)   All of the above.

Your Answer _____

_____

ANSWERS

A–243

(D) All the answer choices are supported by the passage: The subway forever changed life in New York City; New Yorkers were excited about the new subway, even though it shook the streets; the first section of the subway was just a little over nine miles, but it was soon expanded. The correct answer is D.

QUESTIONS

In the world of magazine publishing, several major new periodicals were born in the 1950s. *Flair* offered its version of jazzed-up culture for 50 cents a copy, with a format of accordion inserts, pages with artful cutouts, and a peekaboo cover that was so expensive to produce that it only published a dozen issues before it closed down. For the same 50 cents, the readers of Hugh Hefner's *Playboy* got a foldout of a sexy pin-up Playmate (the first was Marilyn Monroe) and bits of *Playboy* philosophy. Ten years after the first issue, its circulation was 1.1 million. *Mad,* a zany comic that parodied daily life, including itself, was bought by younger readers in similar numbers. *Sports Illustrated* and *Jet* both started out slow but eventually proved to be very popular. Ironically, a spruced-up catalog of TV programs, *TV Guide,* was successful beyond expectations, with 53 regional editions and a circulation of 6.5 million by 1959.

Q–244

The author of the passage would concur on which of the following statements?

(A) Today's popular magazines are more popular than those in circulation during the 1950s.

(B) *TV Guide's* popularity was an unexpected hit.

(C) *Flair* magazine did not succeed because it was too expensive to produce; whereas *Playboy,* which enjoyed immediate success, is still going strong.

(D) B and C, but not A.

Your Answer _____

_____

ANSWERS

A–244

(D) The author of the passage would concur that *TV Guide*'s popularity was an unexpected hit and that *Flair* magazine did not succeed because it was too expensive to produce, whereas *Playboy,* which enjoyed immediate success, is still going strong. The author would not concur that today's popular magazines are more popular than those in circulation during the 1950s; this is not stated in the passage, and most of the periodicals described are still in circulation. Choices B and C are supported by the statement; choice A is not. The correct answer is D.

QUESTIONS

One of the favored courtiers of Queen Elizabeth I of England was the long-lived John Dee (1527–1608). "Doctor Dee," as he was called, enjoyed a special patronage at court, notwithstanding the fact that other members of the court viewed him as an endangered species: official court astrologer. Some years after Dee's death, his son gave all his father's papers and occult equipment to Elias Ashmole, an English antiquarian. In addition to collecting rare old books and writings, Ashmole studied science, including astrology, at Oxford during the English Civil War (1642–1648), wrote horoscopes, and in 1650, was elected Steward of the London Astrologers Society. When Ashmole gave his entire collection, including the Dee materials, to Oxford University in 1682, it became the foundation for the Ashmolean Museum, the earliest science museum to be founded in Britain and named after him.

Q–245

The passage supports which statement(s)?

(A) Through the 17th century, astrology was considered a science.

(B) Court astrologers were waning in popularity by the time of Queen Elizabeth I.

(C) The Ashmolean Museum features a wide array of John Dee's works.

(D) All of the above.

Your Answer _____

ANSWERS

A–245

(D) All the answer choices are supported by the passage: Through the 17th century (1600s), astrology was considered a science; court astrologers were waning in popularity by the time of Queen Elizabeth I (context clue: "an endangered species: official court astrologer"); the Ashmolean Museum features a wide array of John Dee's works. The correct answer is D.

QUESTIONS

Use the following passage to answer questions 246, 247, and 248.

One evening in 1865 when Édouard René Lefèbvre de Laboulaye was hosting a dinner party in honor of the sculptor Frédéric Auguste Bartholdi at his home in Glatigny, France (not far from Versailles), the conversation turned to the idea of the presentation of a gift to America. Ten years later in Paris, Bartholdi and structural engineer Alexandre Gustave Eiffel began work on the gift that had been settled upon: a statue, which Bartholdi entitled *Liberty Enlightening the World.* The statue, whose copper "skin" was created using the repoussé process, was completed in 1884, and on July 4th of that year, a ceremony was held in Paris to officially "present it" to America by the people of France. In early 1885, the complicated dismantling of the statue (into 350 pieces) was undertaken, and the pieces were carefully packed into 214 crates and loaded on board the French frigate *Isère* for shipment to America. In 1877, Richard Morris Hunt had been selected by the American Committee for the Statue of Liberty as the architect of the pedestal that would hold the statue. "The New Colossus," the famous sonnet in tribute to what the statue represents to America and the world, was written by Emma Lazarus in 1883 to adorn the pedestal. The champion fund-raiser for the underwriting of the cost of the pedestal was Joseph Pulitzer, the publisher of the *New York World.* The location chosen for the statue was Bedloe's Island (later renamed Liberty Island), the former location of Fort Wood, a fortress built in 1811 to protect New York Harbor. The Statue of Liberty was officially dedicated on October 28, 1886; it was restored on its centennial in 1986.

Q–246

A good title for this passage might be:

(A) A Brief History of the Statue of Liberty.

(B) Bartholdi, Eiffel, and the Repoussé Process.

(C) France and America: An Ongoing Friendship.

(D) Philanthropy and the Pulitzer Prize.

Your Answer _____

ANSWERS

A–246

(A)   A good title for this passage might be "A Brief History of the Statue of Liberty" (choice A) because that is what the passage is about. Although choices B and C reflect ideas discussed in the passage, they are only mentioned in passing and so would not be appropriate titles for the passage (choices B and C, thus, can be ruled out). Joseph Pulitzer is discussed as a fund-raiser for the project, but the Pulitzer Prize is not mentioned, which rules out choice D. The correct answer is A.

QUESTIONS

Q–247

According to the passage:

(A) The publisher Joseph Pulitzer paid Emma Lazarus to write the poem "New Colossus" for the statue's base.

(B) A little more than two decades passed between the night when the statue was first discussed and its official dedication.

(C) The disassembly and shipment of the statue from France to America was not a complicated procedure.

(D) Bedloe's Island was suggested as the locale for the statue, but because it housed Fort Wood, an alternative spot was chosen.

Your Answer _____

ANSWERS

A–247

(B) According to the passage, 21 years (that is, "a little more than two decades") passed between the night when the statue was first discussed (1865) and its official dedication (1886), so choice B matches the passage. There is no mention of publisher Joseph Pulitzer having paid Emma Lazarus to write "New Colossus" for the statue's base (ruling out choice A). The disassembly (dismantling) and shipment of the statue from France to America was quite a complicated procedure, per the passage's description (ruling out choice C). Bedloe's Island, the former home of Fort Wood, was chosen for the statue's location (ruling out choice D). The correct answer is B. (When you encounter a passage of this length, with three questions listed for it, make sure to read with extra care. After you read the questions and answer choices, go back through the paragraph a second time to note the details that correspond to the questions.)

QUESTIONS

Q–248

The repoussé process is a type of

(A) metalworking.

(B) masonry.

(C) cosmetic.

(D) architecture.

Your Answer _____

ANSWERS

(A) The <u>repoussé</u> <u>process</u> is a type of *metalworking* (choice A). Although this is metallurgical/artistic terminology, you can deduce the correct answer from the passage. The contextual clue is the sentence: "The statue, whose copper 'skin' was created using the repoussé process. . . ." Copper is a metal, so its creation must have involved *metalworking*. No mention is made of any techniques used in *masonry* (concrete) or *architecture* (building), which rules out choices B and D, respectively. "Skin" is in quotes to indicate that it is a thin layer of copper, not actual skin, so *cosmetic* would not be appropriate either (ruling out choice C). The correct answer is A.

QUESTIONS

Peridot is the gem-quality variety of forsteritic olivine. Its name is believed to come from either the Arabic word *faridat,* meaning "gem," or the French word *peritot,* meaning "unclear." Peridot is one of the few gemstones that comes in only one color: green. The intensity of green, which depends on how much iron is contained in the crystal structure of the stone, varies from yellow-green to olive-green to brownish-green. Peridot is also often referred to as the "poor man's emerald." Olivine is a very abundant mineral, but gem-quality peridot is extremely rare. Peridot crystals have been collected from iron-nickel meteorites. The largest cut peridot/olivine is a 310-carat specimen in the Gem and Mineral collection of the Smithsonian Museum in Washington, D.C.

Q–249

The passage supports which statement(s)?

(A) No one knows where the name for peridot comes from.

(B) The mineral source of the peridot is common, but peridot itself occurs infrequently.

(C) Valued for its beautiful green color, peridot is likened by many to emeralds.

(D) B and C, but not A.

Your Answer _____

_____

ANSWERS

A–249

(D) According to the passage, olivine, the mineral source of peridot, is common, but peridot itself occurs infrequently. Peridot is valued for its beautiful green color and is likened by many to emeralds (contextual clue: "referred to as 'the poor man's emerald'.") However, the passage explains that there are two possibilities for the derivation of the name of peridot: one Arabic, and one French. Therefore, choices B and C match the passage, but choice A does not. The correct answer is D.

QUESTIONS

The most important master of the Art Nouveau style of decorative arts during America's Gilded Age was Louis Comfort Tiffany. He was naturally talented in many artistic fields—painting, architecture, landscape, and interior design—and created new styles for furniture, draperies, wallpaper, and rugs. His artistic temperament and vision led him to use various materials, including ornamental bronze, silver, ceramic, enamel, wood, and wrought iron to produce a wide range of items. He is known the world over as America's premier glass artist, in addition to his other contributions to the elegant and graceful Art Nouveau style of ornamentation. His creations are still highly sought after and collected more than 75 years after his death; at auction, prices for some of his works far exceed $1 million.

Q–250

The author of this passage would agree that:

(A) Tiffany might have been important to Art Nouveau, but he was not particularly talented or innovative.

(B) American glass, as an art form, was influenced more by Tiffany than any other artist.

(C) Art Nouveau is prized for its sleek, austere quality.

(D) Auction prices for Tiffany pieces are overinflated.

Your Answer _____

ANSWERS

A–250

(B) The author of this passage would agree that American glass, as an art form, was influenced more by Tiffany than any other artist (choice B). The contextual clue for this is the statement that Tiffany "is known the world over as America's premier glass artist." The complimentary tone of the passage and multiple mentions of his talent and vision indicate that the author considers Tiffany important to Art Nouveau and extremely talented and innovative (ruling out choice A). The passage describes Art Nouveau as "elegant and graceful," not sleek and austere (ruling out choice C). Although auction prices for Tiffany pieces are described as exceeding $1 million in certain instances, nothing indicates that the author considers these prices overinflated; again, the passage continuously praises Tiffany and his work (ruling out choice D). The correct answer is B.

QUESTIONS

Q–251

The lowest, or most specific, level of classification system for living organisms is called a _____.

(A) species

(B) genus

(C) phylum

(D) kingdom

Your Answer _____

_____

Q–252

Which of the choices listed below describes cyclonic winds?

(A) They turn clockwise south of the Equator.

(B) They turn counterclockwise south of the Equator.

(C) There are no cyclonic winds north of the Equator because of the jet stream.

(D) El Niño causes cyclonic winds to become hurricanes.

Your Answer _____

_____

ANSWERS

A–251

(A) Species is the lowest, or most specific, level of classification. Kingdom is the top, or broadest, level. Phylum and genus fall in between, along with other levels. The correct answer is A.

A–252

(A) The Equator divides the earth into the Northern and Southern Hemispheres. In the Southern Hemisphere, cyclonic winds turn clockwise; in the Northern Hemisphere, counterclockwise. The jet stream contributes to weather patterns and climate, but it is not true that it prevents cyclonic winds north of the Equator. Another contributor to weather patterns and climate, El Niño, is more likely to inhibit the formation of hurricanes than to cause them. The correct answer is A.

QUESTIONS

Q–253

_____ is the process by which a solid converts directly to a gas.

(A) Condensation

(B) Combustion

(C) Decomposition

(D) Sublimation

Your Answer _____

Q–254

Heat can be described as a form of

(A) motion.

(B) force.

(C) energy.

(D) calorie.

Your Answer _____

ANSWERS

A–253

(D) The process by which a solid converts directly to a gas, without becoming a liquid, is called sublimation. Condensation is the conversion of a vapor (gas) to a liquid. Combustion is a rapid chemical process that produces heat and light. Decomposition is a process that breaks down matter into simpler parts or forms. The correct answer is D.

A–254

(C) Heat is a form of energy; it is not a form of motion or force. A calorie is a unit of measurement of heat. The correct answer is C.

QUESTIONS

Q–255

At 0°C, the speed of sound is

(A)   1,492 meters per second.

(B)   1,086 feet per second.

(C)   3,500 meters per second.

(D)   186,000 miles per second.

Your Answer _____

Q–256

Of the following metals, which is the best conductor of heat?

(A)   Silver

(B)   Iron

(C)   Copper

(D)   Aluminum

Your Answer _____

ANSWERS

A–255

(B) At 0°C, the speed of sound is 1,086 feet per second (choice B). However, the speed of sound is 1,492 meters per second in seawater (choice A), and 3,500 meters per second in copper (choice C). The speed of light is 186,000 miles per second (choice D). Be careful selecting here, because you may recognize the values in choices A, C, and D. The correct answer is B.

A–256

(A) Of the metals listed, silver is the best conductor of heat because its atoms are closely packed (choice A). Although aluminum expands quickly, it does not conduct heat as well as silver because its atoms are not as closely packed. The correct answer is A.

QUESTIONS

Q–257

The _____ determines the sex of human offspring.

(A) sperm

(B) ovum

(C) mitochondrion

(D) Golgi apparatus

Your Answer _____

Q–258

Mixing all the colors of the spectrum will result in

(A) black.

(B) violet.

(C) yellow.

(D) white.

Your Answer _____

ANSWERS

A–257

(A) The sperm, which carries an X or Y chromosome, determines the sex of human offspring. The ovum (egg cell) normally has one X chromosome. An XX union results in a female; an XY, in a male. Choices C and D are other cell organelles that are not primarily involved in reproduction. The correct answer is A.

A–258

(D) White is a mixture of all the colors of the spectrum; black is the opposite. White light is a reflection of all the spectral colors; in order to see the individual colors, a prism must be used to separate the light into the spectrum's component colors (red, orange, yellow, green, blue, indigo, and violet). The correct answer is D. This is a principle that needs to be understood and memorized, because it could seem that all colors mixed together would result in black, and no color would be white, when actually the opposite is true.

QUESTIONS

Q–259

The _____ areas are typically the hottest parts of a landmass in the summer.

(A)   coastal/ocean

(B)   mountain/hilltop

(C)   interior/inland

(D)   valley/low-lying

Your Answer _____

_____

Q–260

Which of the following is considered an inherited, sex-linked trait?

(A)   Hemophilia

(B)   Eye color

(C)   Height

(D)   Anemia

Your Answer _____

_____

ANSWERS

A–259

(C) Land heats up rapidly in summer and cools off rapidly in winter. As a result, the climate of the continental interior is extremely hot in summer and extremely cold in winter. Coastal and island climates are moderated by the ocean; the seasonal temperatures of mountains and valleys would depend upon their physical position (coastal or inland), although higher and lower altitudes can be cooler and warmer, respectively, than the surrounding area. Nevertheless, it is true that the interior/inland areas are typically the hottest parts of a landmass in the summer (and the coldest part in winter). This question is testing your knowledge of general climate facts; do not be fooled by summer vacations to mountain cabins. The correct answer is C.

A–260

(A) All the choices listed are inherited traits, but only hemophilia, a clotting disorder, is considered to be sex-linked because the gene for it lies on the X chromosome. The correct answer is A.

QUESTIONS

Which of the following is TRUE of concentrated solutions?

(A) They have a high ratio of solute to solvent if there is a large amount of solute dissolved in a small amount of solvent.

(B) They have a low ratio of solute to solvent if there is a large amount of solute dissolved in a small amount of solvent.

(C) They can also be called diluted, depending upon the amount of solute.

(D) They can also be called diluted, depending upon the amount of solvent.

Your Answer _____

_____

The Rh factor is critical when studying

(A) acidity.

(B) alkalinity.

(C) blood.

(D) fingerprints.

Your Answer _____

_____

ANSWERS

A–261

(A) A solution has a high ratio of solute to solvent if there is a large amount of solute dissolved in a small amount of solvent. Such a solution is also said to be concentrated. Therefore, the only choice listed that is TRUE of concentrated solutions is A, which is the correct answer. Note that diluted solutions are the opposite of concentrated solutions, which would automatically rule out choices C and D, allowing you to focus on whether a high (or low) ratio of solute to solvent is the determining factor.

A–262

(C) The Rh factor is an inherited characteristic of the blood; along with blood type (A, B, AB, O), it is critical to hematology (study of the blood/treatment of blood disorders). None of the other choices are related to the Rh factor. The correct answer is C. (Note that acids and bases [alkalines] are measured on the pH scale, but this has nothing to do with the Rh factor.)

QUESTIONS

Q–263

A person who blinks in bright light is exhibiting a response known as a(n) _____.

(A) instinct

(B) habit

(C) phobia

(D) reflex

Your Answer _____

Q–264

Which of the following is/are mainly responsible for causing wind?

(A) Clouds

(B) Unequal heating of air

(C) High humidity

(D) Lightning

Your Answer _____

ANSWERS

A–263

(D) An instinct involves a series of reflexes; in scientific terms, it is not considered a single response. A habit is an acquired trait; a phobia is a type of neurosis related to fear. A reflex is a simple inborn response, such as blinking. The correct answer is D. (Note that "photo" refers to light [photograph, photon, photosynthesis, etc.], but has nothing to do with "phobia"; however, phobia is included as an answer choice to confuse you. The key here is knowing the difference between *instinct* [series of reflexive responses] and *reflex* [single inborn response], from a scientific perspective.)

A–264

(B) Heat always rises. Warm air rises far above the earth's surface, toward a colder region, while cooler (that is, unheated) air flows in to take its place. The result is a horizontal air current that, when close to the earth's surface, is called *wind.* Although all the other choices are weather—or weather-related—phenomena, of the choices listed, only "unequal heating of air" would be an accurate description as responsible for causing wind (choice B).

QUESTIONS

Q–265

_____ appeared most recently on the earth.

(A) Ants

(B) Fish

(C) Frogs

(D) Porpoises

Your Answer _____

Q–266

Which element listed below is part of hemoglobin?

(A) Calcium

(B) Carbon

(C) Iron

(D) Magnesium

Your Answer _____

ANSWERS

A–265

(D) Mammals appeared most recently on the earth; reptiles, insects, fish, and amphibians all have been on the planet far longer. The choices listed include insects (ants), amphibians (frogs), and fish (no reptiles appear on the list). The correct answer is porpoises, which are mammals (choice D). This choice of aquatic mammal is intended to confuse you—many people think porpoises (sometimes called dolphins) are a type of fish; to make it even more confusing there is a type of fish called a dolphin in some areas. The correct answer, however, is still D.

A–266

(C) Iron is a component of hemoglobin, the pigment of red blood cells—it is actually the iron that makes them red. Carbon is a component of all life forms; calcium and magnesium are necessary for strong bones and teeth, as well as other life functions. The correct answer is C.

QUESTIONS

Municipalities add chlorine to drinking-water systems in order to

(A) prevent caries.

(B) improve water taste.

(C) reduce incidence of hydrophobia.

(D) inhibit microbial production.

Your Answer _____

Which of the following are NOT in our solar system?

(A) Pluto, now that it is a dwarf planet

(B) Neptune and Uranus

(C) Nebulae

(D) Ganymede (moon of Jupiter)

Your Answer _____

ANSWERS

A–267

(D) Municipalities add chlorine to drinking-water systems in order to prevent bacteria and other microbes (choice D). Fluoride is added to the drinking-water system to prevent cavities (dental caries). Chlorine is not terribly tasty, but usually the amount used is not noticeable (when municipalities have to add a higher-than-normal amount, residents will be notified). Nothing can be added to the water system to prevent hydrophobia, another name for rabies; it is included to confuse you because "hydro" means water.

A–268

(C) Of all the choices listed, only the nebulae (large clouds of gas and dust located between stars) are outside our solar system. Pluto, although it is now a dwarf planet, is still in our solar system; Neptune and Uranus, though outer planets (farther from the sun), are still in our solar system; Ganymede, the largest satellite (moon) of Jupiter, is part of our solar system, as are the satellites of any planet, including Earth's moon. The question is, essentially, including these facts about the solar system, which is why it identifies Ganymede as a moon of Jupiter. It is really testing your knowledge of the definition of nebulae; if you know that, you know that it is the one choice NOT in our solar system. The correct answer is C.

QUESTIONS

Q–269

Scurvy is the result of a _____ deficiency.

(A) vitamin A

(B) vitamin B

(C) vitamin C

(D) vitamin D and/or calcium

Your Answer _____

_____

Q–270

Which of the following transmits solar energy through space?

(A) Convection

(B) Radiation

(C) Reflection

(D) Refraction

Your Answer _____

_____

ANSWERS

A–269

(C) A vitamin C deficiency, usually the result of a diet not rich in fruits and vegetables, can cause the disease called scurvy. For this reason, sailors were always encouraged to eat plenty of citrus fruits, which kept well on long voyages. (British sailors, in particular, were nicknamed "Limeys" because of the limes kept onboard to encourage vitamin C intake.) Vitamin C is also an immune-system strengthener, among other positive effects it has on the body. Vitamin A deficiencies result in vision problems; vitamin B promotes nerve health and prevents the disease called beri beri; vitamin D and calcium, essential to bone health and strong teeth, also prevent the disease of rickets, which causes children to become bow-legged. The correct answer is C (as in the vitamin!).

A–270

(B) When solar energy moves through space—in the form of ultraviolet rays—it is called *radiation* (choice B). Heat moves by means of conduction, convection, or radiation. Reflection and refraction are both related to light, not heat. The correct answer is B.

QUESTIONS

Q–271

Sound would travel fastest through

(A) a vacuum.

(B) air.

(C) water.

(D) steel.

Your Answer _____

Q–272

Which of the following statements is/are true about metal alloys?

(A) Some of them are naturally occurring.

(B) They are stronger, harder, and lighter than their component metals.

(C) They are man-made.

(D) B and C, but not A.

Your Answer _____

ANSWERS

A–271

(D) Sound travels fastest through the densest materials because molecules in heavier materials are packed closer together than they are in lighter materials, allowing sound vibrations to transmit more rapidly. Sound does not travel through a vacuum, ruling out choice A. Of the other choices listed, steel is the densest material. The correct answer is D.

A–272

(D) Alloys are metals that are fused together to make them stronger, harder, and lighter than their component metals. Brass is an alloy of copper and zinc; bronze is an alloy of copper and tin; steel is an alloy of iron and carbon (plus other metals, at times, such as chromium steel). Alloys must be created; they never occur in nature. Therefore, choices B and C are true, but choice A is not true. The correct answer is D.

QUESTIONS

Q–273

_____ is the process of evaporating a liquid by heating it, and then cooling it by means of condensation.

(A) Carbonation

(B) Chlorination

(C) Distillation

(D) Ozonation

Your Answer _____

Q–274

Which of the following are examples of bases?

(A) Ammonia

(B) Baking soda

(C) Vinegar

(D) A and B, but not C

Your Answer _____

ANSWERS

A–273

(C) The process of evaporating a liquid by heating it, and then cooling it by means of condensation, is called distillation (choice C). The other choices refer to the processes of adding carbon, chlorine, and ozone, respectively, for varied purposes. If you read carefully, you can eliminate choices A, B, and D to deduce that C is the correct answer, even if you don't know what distillation means.

A–274

(D) Ammonia and baking soda (that is, sodium bicarbonate, commonly used as an antacid) are both examples of bases; however, vinegar contains acetic acid. Therefore, A and B both are bases, but C is not. The correct answer is D.

QUESTIONS

Q–275

Which of the following are parts of the human eye?

(A)   Pupil, iris, cornea

(B)   Lens, retina, sclera

(C)   Cochlea, tympanum, anvil

(D)   A and B, but not C

Your Answer _____

Q–276

Select the choice that shows the three most common elements in commercial fertilizers:

(A)   Nitrogen, phosphorus and potassium

(B)   Calcium, iron, and phosphorus

(C)   Iron, magnesium, and sulfur

(D)   Nitrogen, phosphorus, and sulfur

Your Answer _____

ANSWERS

A–275

(D) The pupil, iris, cornea, lens, retina, and sclera all are parts of the human eye. The cochlea, tympanum, and anvil all are parts of the human ear, not the human eye. Therefore, choices A and B are true, but choice C is not true. The correct answer is D.

A–276

(A) Nitrogen, phosphorus, and potassium are the three most common elements in commercial fertilizers. Of these three, plants need nitrogen the most; they also need phosphorus and potassium. The elements in the other choices—calcium, iron, magnesium, and sulfur—are not needed by plants, so the companies that manufacture fertilizers do not include them in their products. The correct answer is A.

QUESTIONS

Q–277

All of the following pertain to light EXCEPT

(A) reflection.

(B) convection.

(C) refraction.

(D) illumination.

Your Answer _____

_____

Q–278

"At one time Alaska had a tropical climate." This statement is true because

(A) much of Alaska is in the tundra biome.

(B) Alaska has coal deposits.

(C) Alaska is covered with ice through much of the winter.

(D) Alaska is famous for its diamond mines.

Your Answer _____

_____

ANSWERS

A–277

(B) Convection is one of the ways that heat moves; it does not pertain to light. Reflection is one of the results when light hits a surface (the other is incidental light). Illumination is visibility by means of reflected light. Refraction is the bending of light (one type of electromagnetic wave) as it passes from one medium to another. A reflection is what we see in the mirror; an illumination is anything we can see because it is lit; refraction is used by ophthalmologists to test the human eye. Choices A, C, and D pertain to light, but choice B does not. The question specifies that all the statements pertain to light EXCEPT one, so the correct answer is B.

A–278

(B) "At one time Alaska had a tropical climate." This statement is true because Alaska has coal deposits. Coal deposits were formed when layers of giant ferns—as well as other types of vegetation—were compressed into layers of coal by the earth's movement. Thus, its coal deposits tell today's scientists that Alaska must have had a tropical climate at some point in time. The correct answer is B. (Note that, although choices A and C are factual, they do not prove the statement in the question to be true.)

QUESTIONS

Q–279

The mass of an object has been doubled. What effect will this have on its acceleration due to gravity?

(A) Its acceleration due to gravity will be unchanged.

(B) Its acceleration due to gravity will be halved.

(C) Its acceleration due to gravity will be doubled.

(D) Its acceleration due to gravity will be tripled.

Your Answer _____

_____

Q–280

All of the following are true about acids and bases EXCEPT

(A) Acids and bases neutralize each other to form a salt and water.

(B) Acids are corrosive and change litmus paper to a pink-red color.

(C) Bases react with fat to form soaps.

(D) Litmus paper is naturally blue; a base will turn it white.

Your Answer _____

_____

ANSWERS

A–279

(A) All freely falling objects, regardless of their masses near the earth, fall toward the earth with equal acceleration. So, any two objects at rest that begin to fall at exactly the same instant will have equal velocities at the end of any given time interval. The correct answer is A. The other choices are designed to confuse you; the key concept here is understanding that the acceleration would not change.

A–280

(D) Acids and bases neutralize each other to form a salt and water; acids are corrosive and change litmus paper to a pink-red color; bases react with fat to form soaps. However, litmus paper is not naturally blue; it turns blue in the presence of a base. Choices A, B, and C are true; choice D is not. The question specifies that all the statements are true EXCEPT one, so the correct answer is D.

QUESTIONS

Q-281

The pancreas is part of which system(s)?

(A) Immune and lymphatic

(B) Digestive

(C) Endocrine

(D) B and C, but not A

Your Answer _____

Q-282

The three states of matter are

(A) solid, liquid, gas.

(B) solid, fluid, gas.

(C) atom, molecule, element.

(D) element, compound, solution.

Your Answer _____

ANSWERS

A–281

(D) The pancreas is a gland that produces insulin, which is necessary to process sugars and starches. (Problems with insulin production can lead to diabetes and obesity.) All glands are part of the endocrine system; each gland's function determines its role in other body systems. Because pancreatic function is necessary to process certain foods, it is also part of the digestive system. (Disease of the pancreas is usually referred to as pancreatitis.) It is not part of the immune and lymphatic systems. Therefore, choices B and C are true, but choice A is not true. The correct answer is D.

A–282

(A) The three states of matter are solid, liquid, and gas (choice A). This is just a scientific fact that needs to be memorized. Solids have definite size and shape. Liquids have definite volume, but no definite shape; they take the shape of the container they are in. Gases have neither definite volume nor definite shape; they fill the container they are in.

QUESTIONS

Q–283

The scientific method involves utilization and/or testing of

(A)   laws and principles.

(B)   theories and experiments.

(C)   observations and hypotheses.

(D)   All of the above.

Your Answer _____

_____

Q–284

Which of the statements below are accurate descriptions of the earth's atmosphere?

(A)   It consists mostly of nitrogen, some oxygen, a small amount of carbon dioxide, and trace amounts of other gases.

(B)   It is a mixture of gases, liquid droplets, and minute solid particles.

(C)   It is made up of mostly ozone and some nitrogen, water vapor, and compressible argon.

(D)   A and B, but not C.

Your Answer _____

_____

ANSWERS

A–283

(D) The scientific method involves utilization and/or testing of laws and principles, theories and experiments, and observations and hypotheses. The correct answer is D (all of the above).

A–284

(D) Earth's atmosphere is a mixture of gases, liquid droplets (water vapor), and minute solid particles (dust). By volume, it consists mostly of nitrogen (approx. 78%), some oxygen (approx. 21%), a small amount of carbon dioxide (approx. 0.3%), and trace amounts of other rare gases, such as neon, xenon, krypton, and helium. It is NOT true that the atmosphere is made up of mostly ozone, and some nitrogen, water vapor, and compressible argon. (Note that the hole in the ozone layer is a key aspect of climate change and global warming.) Therefore, choices A and B are true, but choice C is not true. The correct answer is D.

QUESTIONS

Q–285

Which of the following are NOT classified as world biomes?

(A) Desert, grasslands, taiga

(B) Chaparral, savanna, tundra

(C) Coral reef, polar ice caps, sea bed

(D) Deciduous forest, rainforest, alpine

Your Answer _____

Q–286

Which of the following are examples of acids?

(A) Lemon juice

(B) Pure water

(C) Vinegar

(D) A and C, but not B

Your Answer _____

ANSWERS

A–285

(C)   Although they contain communities of life, choice C (coral reef, polar ice caps, sea bed) does not list specific world biomes, which are major ecological community types in specific climate zones. Choices A, B, and D all represent world biomes; the question asks which choice does not contain biomes, so the correct answer is C.

A–286

(D)   Lemon juice (contains citric acid) and vinegar (contains acetic acid) are both examples of acids; pure water is neutral (neither acid nor base). Thus, choices A and C are true, but choice B is not. The correct answer is D. (Note that acids are usually easier to identify than bases because their names appear with the word acid [for example, sulfuric acid, nitric acid, hydrochloric acid, etc.].)

QUESTIONS

Q–287

All of the following are metal alloys EXCEPT

(A) brass.

(B) bronze.

(C) steel.

(D) titanium.

Your Answer _____

Q–288

The process that changes a liquid to a gas is called

(A) sublimation.

(B) evaporation.

(C) dehydration.

(D) condensation.

Your Answer _____

ANSWERS

A–287

(D) Brass is an alloy of copper and zinc; bronze is an alloy of copper and tin; steel is an alloy of iron and carbon (with other elements added at times). Titanium, however, is a metallic element, not an alloy. The question states that all are metal alloys EXCEPT one, so the correct answer is D.

A–288

(B) Sublimation (choice A) is the conversion of a solid directly to a gas; evaporation is the conversion of a liquid to a gas (choice B); dehydration is the removal of water—that is, hydrogen and oxygen (choice C); condensation is the conversion of a gas to a liquid (choice D). The correct answer is B.

QUESTIONS

Q–289

Heat is transferred from one place to another by

(A) conduction, convection, or radiation.

(B) conduction, convection, or condensation.

(C) conduction, convection, or evaporation.

(D) conduction, convection, or sublimation.

Your Answer _____

Q–290

Which of the following best describes what happens when a salt is dissolved in water?

(A) It causes the water to freeze and leave the salt.

(B) It causes little or no difference in the freezing point.

(C) It causes a decrease in the freezing point of the solution.

(D) It causes an increase in the freezing point of the solution.

Your Answer _____

ANSWERS

A–289

(A) Heat can be transferred from one place to another
by conduction, convection, or radiation (choice A).
Condensation, evaporation, and sublimation do not involve
the transfer of heat from one place to another, so choices B,
C, and D all are incorrect, even though they include
conduction and convection. Remember that choices with
partially accurate information are designed to confuse
you—you must always read carefully to ensure that your
choice is completely accurate, especially when you think
other choices may be partially right.

A–290

(C) When a salt is dissolved in water, the freezing point
of the solution decreases (choice C). This happens because
the salt increases the solution's specific gravity, lowering its
freezing point. All the other choices are incorrect.

QUESTIONS

Q–291

Which correctly expresses Ohm's Law?

(A)   amperes = current × resistance

(B)   voltage = current × resistance

(C)   voltage = resistance ÷ amperes

(D)   ohms = voltage ÷ current

Your Answer _____

_____

Q–292

Power is measured in _____.

(A)   hertz

(B)   amperes

(C)   volts

(D)   watts

Your Answer _____

_____

ANSWERS

A–291

(B) Although the other choices all contain electrical/electronic terminology, the only choice that accurately represents Ohm's Law is (B), voltage = current × resistance.

A–292

(D) Watts measure electrical power. Hertz measure cycles per second. Amperes measure the strength, or intensity, of electrical current. Volts measure electrical pressure. The correct answer is D.

QUESTIONS

Q-293

"Two coils of wire linked by an iron core and used to increase and decrease AC voltage(s)" is a description of

(A) a transformer.

(B) an inductor.

(C) a transistor

(D) a capacitor.

Your Answer _____

Q-294

If a battery contains 12 cells, how many volts could it have?

(A) 9

(B) 12

(C) 18

(D) 30

Your Answer _____

ANSWERS

A–293

(A) The definition correctly describes a transformer (choice A). An inductor is a single coil of wire that creates a magnetic field when current passes through it. A transistor amplifies current. A capacitor stores electric charge.

A–294

(C) A cell contains approximately 1.2–2.2 volts. Therefore, if a battery has 12 cells, multiply 12 by a number that falls within that voltage range:

$12 \times 1.2 = 14.4$

$12 \times 1.5 = 18$

$12 \times 1.8 = 21.6$

$12 \times 2.2 = 26.4$

The only choice that would work is 18 (choice C).

QUESTIONS

A number 6 wire is _____ than a number 36 wire.

(A) larger in diameter

(B) shorter in length

(C) longer in length

(D) smaller in diameter

Your Answer _____

If a resistor is marked 3K-Ω, which of the values below could it have?

(A) 300 watts

(B) 3,000 watts

(C) 300 ohms

(D) 3,000 ohms

Your Answer _____

ANSWERS

A–295

(A) The higher the gauge number of a wire, the smaller its diameter, so a 6 wire is larger in diameter than a 36 wire (choice A). It might seem that the opposite would be true, so be sure to get these facts straight before test day.

A–296

(D) "K" means kilo, which equals 1,000. A 3K-Ω resistor's value would be: $3 \times 1,000$ ohms; or, 3,000 ohms (choice D). Watts are the incorrect unit measurement, so even though choice B has the right value (3,000), it is incorrect. Ohms measure resistance. The correct answer is D. Notice that this question tests values, measurement units, and symbols (that is, Ω = ohm and K = kilo).

QUESTIONS

Q–297

Which of the following is NOT an equivalent term for voltage?

(A) Electromotive force

(B) Capacitive reactance

(C) Potential difference

(D) Electrical pressure

Your Answer _____

Q–298

The property of a circuit that opposes any change in current is called _____.

(A) resistance

(B) conductance

(C) capacitance

(D) inductance

Your Answer _____

ANSWERS

A–297

(B) Capacitive reactance is not an equivalent term for voltage, but all the others are. The correct answer is B. (Note that capacitive reactance is related to capacitance, which is the property of a circuit that opposes any change in voltage, but it is not the same as voltage.)

A–298

(D) Resistance is the property of a circuit that opposes the flow of electrons. Conductance is the property of a circuit that allows for the flow of electrons. Capacitance is the property of a circuit that opposes any change in voltage. Inductance is the property of a circuit that opposes any change in current. The correct answer is D.

QUESTIONS

Q–299

Which property accomplishes the opposite of what resistance accomplishes?

(A) Capacitance

(B) Impedance

(C) Conductance

(D) Reactance

Your Answer _____

Q–300

An ionic hair dryer has a rating of 1,800 watts. If it is operated at 120 volts, how much current will this small appliance draw?

(A) 0.067 amps

(B) 150 amps

(C) 15 amps

(D) 216,000 amps

Your Answer _____

ANSWERS

A–299

(C) The property that accomplishes the opposite of what resistance accomplishes is conductance. Resistance opposes the flow of electrons in a circuit; conductance allows them. Capacitance opposes change in voltage in a circuit. Impedance is the total opposition to current flow in a circuit. The correct answer is C.

A–300

(C) To determine the current requirement of any appliance, use the power law: power = current × voltage ($P = I \times E$). Substitute the values we know into the formula: $1{,}800 = I \times 120$. Divide 1,800 by 120 to determine the value of I: $1{,}800 \div 120 = 15$. The correct answer is C. (The specification that the hair dryer is ionic has nothing to do with obtaining the correct answer. Ionic hair dryers simply reduce frizz.)

QUESTIONS

Q-301

Which of the following describes the piezoelectric effect?

(A) The process of transmitting voice by varying the height of the carrier wave.

(B) The escape of electrons from a surface because of the presence of heat.

(C) The property of a magnetic substance that causes magnetization to lag behind the force producing it.

(D) The property of certain crystalline substances to change shape when a voltage is impressed upon them.

Your Answer _____

Q-302

The symbol above represents a(n)

(A) iron core choke.

(B) tetrode tube.

(C) radio frequency coil.

(D) potentiometer.

Your Answer _____

ANSWERS

A–301

(D) Piezoelectric effect can be defined as the property of certain crystalline substances to change shape when a voltage is impressed upon them. The process of transmitting voice by varying the height of the carrier wave is amplitude modulation. The escape of electrons from a surface because of the presence of heat is thermoionic emission. The property of a magnetic substance that causes magnetization to lag behind the force producing it is hysteresis. The correct answer is D. There's just no getting around memorizing these principles. . . .

A–302

(A) The symbol shown represents an iron core choke. The correct answer is A. Note that choice C is intended to confuse you because it contains the word *coil* and so it "looks" like it could be correct. There is no way around memorizing these symbols!

QUESTIONS

Q–303

A carbon resistor is marked the following color bands: red, red, red, gold. What is its value and tolerance?

(A) 222 Ω ± 5%

(B) 22 Ω ± 5%

(C) 220 Ω ± 5%

(D) 2,200 Ω ± 5%

Your Answer _____

Q–304

A 70/30 rosin core would have a composition of

(A) 70% rosin, 30% tin.

(B) 70% rosin, 30 % silver.

(C) 70% tin, 30% lead.

(D) 70% lead, 30% tin.

Your Answer _____

ANSWERS

A–303

(D) First, read the resistor code: The first two bands indicate numbers; the third band is the multiplier (or number of zeros that are written after the first two numbers); the fourth band indicates the resistor's tolerance. Following the color code specified, the value of this resistor is 2,200 ohms ± 5%. Red, representing a number value of 2 and a multiplier value of 100 (that is, two zeros to write after the first two numbers) would indicate a resistor coded like this:

2	2
Band 1 − Red	Band 2 − Red
00	±5%
Band 3 − Red	Band 4 − Gold

The tolerance of a fixed carbon resistor is a ± value. Gold represents 5% tolerance. The correct answer is D.

A–304

(C) Rosin is a substance in the center of solder; it is added to aid in the soldering process. The amount of silver present in rosin is minute, so choices A and B cannot be correct. The first number gives the percentage of tin, and the second number gives the percentage of lead: 70% tin, 30% lead (choice C). Choice D gives the correct percentages and the correct substances, but the order is reversed.

QUESTIONS

Q–305

The primary of a transformer is connected to 120 volts, and the voltage across the secondary of the same transformer is 120 volts. What turns ratio does this transformer have?

(A) 1:1

(B) 0:1

(C) 1:2

(D) Cannot determine from the information given

Your Answer _____

Q–306

From the diagrams below, identify the correct schematic symbol for a variable capacitor.

(A)

(B)

(C) ———ᐰᐰᐰ———

(D) ⊥
     ―ᐬ―

Your Answer _____

ANSWERS

A–305

(A) If the primary and the secondary of a transformer have the same voltage, the turns ratio is 1:1 (choice A). The other choices all are incorrect. Remember to always be wary of choices that say the answer cannot be determined from the information given.

A–306

(B) Choice A is the symbol for a potentiometer, which is a variable resistor; choice C is the symbol for a fixed resistor; choice D is the symbol for a fixed capacitor. The correct symbol for a variable capacitor is choice B. Note that the variable symbols are designated by arrows that are added to the fixed symbols. Knowing this will enable you to automatically eliminate the fixed symbols (choices C and D), and then you just have to identify which symbol designates a capacitor, and which designates a resistor.

QUESTIONS

Q–307

A pentode tube is represented by:

(A)

(C)

(B)

(D)

Your Answer _____

Q–308

If all resistors (R_1, R_2, R_3) in a series circuit equal 750 Ω, what is the total resistance of the circuit?

(A) 7.5 kilowatts

(B) 7,500 watts

(C) 2.25 ohms

(D) 2,250 ohms

Your Answer _____

ANSWERS

A–307

(C) Choice C represents a pentode tube. Choices A, B, and D represent tetrode, diode, and triode tubes, respectively. This is basic symbol identification. If you know that choice B is a diode, all you need to do is count the additional dashed lines to determine the correct answer. Choice C has three dashed lines, added to the diode, which makes it a pentode.

A–308

(D) In any series circuit, total resistance is equal to the sum of the individual resistors:

$$R_T = R_1 + R_2 + R_3 + \cdots + R_n$$

The question specified that each resistor (R_1, R_2, R_3) in a series circuit equals 750 Ω. Substitute the given values into the formulas:

$$R_T = 750 + 750 + 750$$

$$R_T = 2{,}250 \ \Omega$$

The correct answer is D. This question tests knowledge of units, formulas, and symbols. Ω is the symbol for ohms, which measure resistance; watts measure power.

QUESTIONS

Q–309

The unit of conductance is known as the _____.

(A) siemen

(B) ohm

(C) watt

(D) solder

Your Answer _____

Q–310

What does the formula below represent?

$$X_c = \frac{1}{2\pi f C}$$

(A) Conductance

(B) Capacitive reactance

(C) Resistance

(D) Inductive reactance

Your Answer _____

ANSWERS

A–309

(A) The siemen is the unit of conductance. The ohm is the unit of resistance, and the watt is the unit of power. Solder, which is unrelated to this question, is included to cause confusion because the symbol for siemen is S.

A–310

(B) The formula listed represents capacitive reactance (choice B). Note that in the formula, f = frequency expressed in hertz; C = capacitance expressed in farads; X_c = capacitive reactance expressed in ohms (X_c is opposition to current flow). Remember that formulas just need to be memorized!

QUESTIONS

Q–311

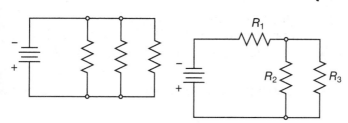

Identify these two diagrams.

(A)   Fig. 1 is a parallel circuit; fig. 2 is a series-parallel circuit.

(B)   Fig. 1 is a series-parallel circuit; fig. 2 is a parallel circuit.

(C)   Fig. 1 is a parallel circuit; fig. 2 is a series circuit.

(D)   Fig. 1 is a series circuit; fig. 2 is a parallel circuit.

Your Answer _____

Q–312

What is the term for changing alternating current to direct current?

(A)   Rectification

(B)   Alteration

(C)   Inductance

(D)   Capacitance

Your Answer _____

ANSWERS

A–311

(A) The diagrams shown are of a parallel circuit (fig. 1) and a series-parallel circuit (fig. 2). Choices B, C, and D are listed to cause confusion. The correct answer is A.

A–312

(A) Changing alternating current to direct current is called rectification (choice A). Alteration (choice B) is not an electric/electronic term. Inductance is the circuit property that opposes any change in current (choice C); capacitance is the circuit property that opposes any change in voltage (choice D). The correct answer is A.

QUESTIONS

Q–313

The maximum frequency at which radar can operate is

(A) 500,000 MHz.

(B) 100,000 Hz.

(C) 100,000 kHz.

(D) 100,000 MHz.

Your Answer _____

_____

Q–314

With respect to the speed of sound, radio waves travel

(A) slower.

(B) faster.

(C) at the same speed.

(D) sometimes slower and sometimes faster, depending upon frequency.

Your Answer _____

_____

ANSWERS

A–313

(D) The maximum frequency at which radar can operate is 100,000 MHz (choice D). Choice A is too high; choices B and C are too low. The correct answer is D.

A–314

(B) Radio waves travel faster than the speed of sound (choice B). The other choices are incorrect. This question is designed to test your knowledge of these rules, which simply must be memorized!

QUESTIONS

Q–315

A SIM card can be found in which of the following?

(A)   Analog cellphones

(B)   e-reader devices

(C)   MP3 players

(D)   Newer digital cellphones

Your Answer _____

_____

Q–316

What will the result be if an incandescent light bulb is operated at less than its rated voltage?

(A)   It will burn brighter and last longer.

(B)   It will burn brighter, but not last as long.

(C)   It will burn dimmer and last longer.

(D)   It will burn dimmer, but last longer.

Your Answer _____

_____

ANSWERS

A–315

(D) Newer digital cellphones have SIM cards, which contain information, such as the phone number, billing information, and address book. SIM stands for subscriber identity module; the single card, which can be exchanged from one phone to another, makes it easier for users when they buy new phones. The correct answer is D. The other devices do not require SIM cards.

A–316

(C) If an incandescent light bulb is operated at less than its rated voltage, it will burn dimmer and last longer. This is because the full potential of the bulb is not being used. The correct answer is C (none of the other choices is accurate).

QUESTIONS

Q–317

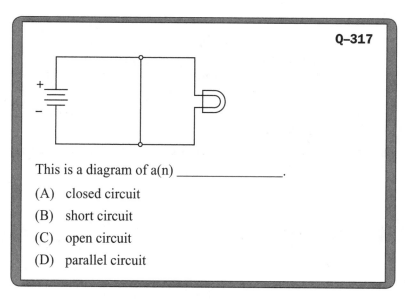

This is a diagram of a(n) _____.

(A) closed circuit

(B) short circuit

(C) open circuit

(D) parallel circuit

Your Answer _____

Q–318

The color of neutral wire is always

(A) gray.

(B) white.

(C) natural.

(D) either B or C.

Your Answer _____

ANSWERS

A–317

(B) The diagram shown is a short circuit. The vertical line between the two dots is the short. A short circuit has a path of low resistance to electron flow, usually created when a low-resistance wire is placed across the consuming device. The correct answer is B.

A–318

(D) The color of neutral wire is always white or natural (choice D). Gray is not a neutral wire color.

QUESTIONS

Q–319

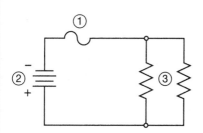

In this diagram, which of the numbered locations indicates the fuse?

(A) 1

(B) 2

(C) 3

(D) 2 or 3, but not 1

Your Answer _____

Q–320

If you need to measure electrical power, which of the following should you use?

(A) Wattmeter

(B) Ohmmmeter

(C) Potentiometer

(D) Voltmeter

Your Answer _____

ANSWERS

A–319

(A) According to the labels on this diagram, the fuse is in 1 (choice A). Choice B (label 2) is a battery, and choice C (label 3) is the resistors. Because neither B nor C is correct, and A is correct, choice D is also incorrect. The correct answer is A.

A–320

(A) A wattmeter is used to measure electrical power because watts are the units of measurement for power (choice A). This question is used to test your knowledge of units; if you know that watts measure power, then wattmeter has to be the correct answer. Likewise, voltmeters measure volts and ohmmeters measure ohms. Potentiometers, however, are variable resistors. The correct answer is A.

QUESTIONS

Q–321

Of the choices listed below, the best component for the core of an electromagnetic-induction device would be
_____.

(A) aluminum

(B) brass

(C) iron

(D) silver

Your Answer _____

Q–322

Which of the definitions below describes permeability?

(A) It is force-field intensity measurement.

(B) It is a unit of measurement of magnetism.

(C) It is the property that makes a magnet permanent.

(D) It is the ease with which magnetic lines of force distribute themselves throughout a material.

Your Answer _____

ANSWERS

A–321

(C) Of the choices listed, iron would be the best component of the core of an electromagnetic-induction device (choice C). Iron is easily magnetized and demagnetized, so it would work better in this type of device than the other choices.

A–322

(D) Permeability is the ease with which magnetic lines of force distribute themselves throughout a material (choice D). The other choices do not describe permeability.

QUESTIONS

Q–323

Traditional color television uses three basic colors to produce the full color range required for a good picture. Which of the following represent these three colors?

(A) Cyan, yellow, magenta

(B) Red, yellow, blue

(C) Red, green, blue

(D) Orange, green, purple

Your Answer _____

Q–324

The magnetron and klystron can be described as

_____.

(A) two types of oscillators used for microwave generation

(B) two types of low-frequency transmitters

(C) two types of audio-frequency amplifiers

(D) two types of permeability detectors

Your Answer _____

ANSWERS

A–323

(C) The three basic colors used by traditional color television are red, green, blue (abbreviated RGB). Computer monitors use RGB as well. The correct answer is C. The other choices are incorrect, but choice A (with the addition of black) is used in print, and some computer monitors used for graphic design in print output can be calibrated to CMYK (cyan, magenta, yellow, black). The correct answer is C.

A–324

(A) The magnetron and klystron are two types of oscillators used for microwave generation (choice A). Although the klystron is a frequency source in microwaves, the other answers are incorrect.

QUESTIONS

Q–325

To prevent a short circuit, use a(n)

(A) fuse.

(B) insulator.

(C) solder.

(D) neutral wire.

Your Answer _____

Q–326

If you use insulated fittings to splice wires, you do not need to _____.

(A) twist the wires together

(B) clean the wires

(C) solder the wires together

(D) remove the wires' plastic coating

Your Answer _____

ANSWERS

A–325

(A) Using a fuse prevents short circuits, which have a path of low resistance to electron flow and are usually created when a low-resistance wire is placed across the consuming device. The correct answer is A; the other choices are not related to preventing short circuits.

A–326

(C) Insulated fittings replace soldering, so if you use these fittings to splice wires, you do not need to solder the wires together. The correct answer is C. The use of insulated fittings is not related to the other choices, so they are not correct.

QUESTIONS

Q–327

With respect to the speed of light, radio waves travel

(A) faster.

(B) slower.

(C) at the same speed.

(D) sometimes faster and sometimes slower, depending upon frequency.

Your Answer _____

Q–328

Provided that the capacitor is the same, an increase of the frequency will cause a(n) _____ of the capacitive reactance.

(A) increase

(B) decrease

(C) increase or decrease, depending upon conductance

(D) increase or decrease, depending upon inductance

Your Answer _____

ANSWERS

A–327

(C) Radio waves travel at the same speed as the speed of light (choice C). The other choices all are incorrect. This question is designed to test your knowledge of these rules, which simply must be memorized!

A–328

(B) Provided that the capacitor is the same, an increase of the frequency will cause a decrease of the capacitive reactance (choice B). As long as the frequency stays the same: If capacitance decreases, capacitive reactance will increase, and if capacitance increases, capacitive reactance will decrease. As long as the capacitor stays the same: If frequency decreases, capacitive reactance will increase, and if frequency increases, capacitive reactance will decrease.

QUESTIONS

Q–329

Which best describes the voltage across all branches of a parallel circuit?

(A) Voltage across all branches of a parallel circuit is the same.

(B) Voltage across all branches of a parallel circuit is different.

(C) Voltage across all branches of a parallel circuit varies, dependent upon resistance.

(D) Voltage across all branches of a parallel circuit varies, dependent upon current.

Your Answer _____

Q–330

What does the formula below represent?

$$G = \frac{A}{pL}$$

(A) Inductance

(B) Impedance

(C) Resonance

(D) Conductance

Your Answer _____

ANSWERS

A–329

(A) Voltage across all branches of a parallel circuit is the same because all branches are connected across the voltage source. The other answers are incorrect. Here again is a rule that just needs to be memorized. The correct answer is A.

A–330

(D) The formula listed represents conductance (choice D). Remember that formulas just need to be memorized!

QUESTIONS

Q–331

Which auto parts are no longer used because of fuel injectors?

(A) Throttles

(B) Crankshafts

(C) Carburetors

(D) Pistons

Your Answer _____

Q–332

The _____ ignites the fuel and air mixture.

(A) accelerator

(B) spark plug

(C) flywheel

(D) push rod

Your Answer _____

ANSWERS

A–331

(C) Carburetors mechanically mix fuel and air but are no longer necessary because of fuel injectors. (They can be found on cars made in or prior to 1990.) The other parts are all still in use. Throttles cause the transfer of fuel, formerly through the carburetor, and now electronically. Crankshafts and pistons work together within the engine's cylinders. The correct answer is C.

A–332

(B) Although the flywheel and push rod are both engine parts, it is the spark plug that ignites the fuel and air mixture, so the correct answer is (B). "Spark" and "ignite" can be used as clues for those who recognize that choices (C) and (D) are also engine components. Accelerator is included as a deliberately confusing answer for test takers with no automotive knowledge.

QUESTIONS

Q–333

Which is NOT part of a car's brake system?

(A) Brake lock

(B) Brake line

(C) Brake shoe

(D) Brake fluid

Your Answer _____

_____

Q–334

On an automatic transmission indicator, *P* means that the transmission is

(A) running at its highest speed.

(B) running at its lowest speed.

(C) ready to tow (pull) heavy loads.

(D) locked to prevent the car from moving.

Your Answer _____

_____

ANSWERS

A–333

(A) There is no such thing as a "brake lock" per se, but the other choices are all part of brake systems. Don't be fooled by antilock brake systems (ABS), which keep the wheels, not the brakes, from locking up. The correct answer is A.

A–334

(D) On an automatic transmission indicator, *P* stands for Park, which means that the transmission is locked, the wheels cannot roll, and so the car cannot move (choice D). None of the other choices would be correct. Memorizing the automatic indicator letters and manual shift numbers is key to success on this part of the test.

QUESTIONS

Q–335

In addition to coolant (antifreeze), all of the following work together as part of the engine's cooling system EXCEPT for the

(A) radiator.

(B) water jackets.

(C) water pump.

(D) air-conditioning.

Your Answer _____

Q–336

In rear-wheel drive

(A) the rear wheels push the car.

(B) the rear wheels pull the car.

(C) the front wheels push the car, while the rear wheels pull it.

(D) the driveshaft extends from the rear axle to the transmission.

Your Answer _____

ANSWERS

A–335

(D) The radiator, water jackets, water pump, and coolant (antifreeze) all work together as part of the engine's cooling system. Air-conditioning cools the interior of the vehicle but has nothing to do with cooling the engine. The correct answer is D. Read carefully—the correct answer has to be "wrong" because the question specifies "all of the following EXCEPT for."

A–336

(A) In rear-wheel drive, the rear wheels push the car (choice A), and the driveshaft extends from the transmission to the rear axle. In front-wheel drive, the front wheels pull the car, and the driveshaft extends from the transmission to the front axle. In all-wheel drive (four-wheel drive), all wheels push and pull the car simultaneously, and the driveshaft extends from the transmission to both axles. Choices B, C, and D are incorrect; notice that choice D reverses the position of the driveshaft in rear-wheel drive—the driveshaft always extends from the transmission to the axle(s), regardless of the type of drive system. The correct answer is A.

QUESTIONS

Q–337

The catalytic converter _____.

(A) oxidizes hydrocarbons into water vapor and carbon dioxide

(B) oxidizes carbon monoxide into water vapor and carbon dioxide

(C) controls nitrogen oxides

(D) A and B, but not C

Your Answer _____

Q–338

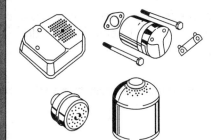

The diagram shows examples of which automotive part?

(A) Filters

(B) Mufflers

(C) Carburetors

(D) Cylinders

Your Answer _____

ANSWERS

A–337

(D) Catalytic converters oxidize hydrocarbons and carbon monoxide into water vapor and carbon dioxide (choices A and B) but do not control nitrogen oxides (choice C). Therefore, choices A and B apply to catalytic converters, but choice C does not. The correct answer is D.

A–338

(B) The diagram shows examples of mufflers that are used on small gasoline engines (choice B). The other choices do not appear in this diagram.

QUESTIONS

Q–339

The right side of the car's engine

(A) is to the right when you stand in front of the car and look toward the engine.

(B) is to the right when you sit in the driver's seat and look forward.

(C) is the side where the distributor is.

(D) depends upon the automotive manufacturer.

Your Answer _____

_____

Q–340

A(n) _____ is used to diagnose problems in automotive ignition systems.

(A) magnetoscope

(B) kinetoscope

(C) oscilloscope

(D) endoscope

Your Answer _____

_____

ANSWERS

A–339

(B) When you sit in the driver's seat and look forward, the side to your right is the right side of the car's engine. This method is used by all manufacturers (choice B). This is something you just need to memorize; all the other choices are incorrect and are listed to create confusion.

A–340

(C) An oscilloscope is a special type of voltmeter that displays traces and oscillations on a TV-like picture tube. Because it is able to show the rapid changes in voltage that occur in the ignition system, it is helpful in diagnosing problems. The correct answer is C. The other choices have nothing to do with automotive ignition systems.

QUESTIONS

Q–341

First gear on a manual transmission is the same as which automatic transmission indicator?

(A) L

(B) 1

(C) L_0

(D) All of the above

Your Answer _____

_____

ANSWERS

A–341

(D) First gear on a manual transmission is the same as Low on automatic transmissions. Depending upon the age of the vehicle, Low can be indicated by L, L_0, or 1; therefore, all the choices listed are accurate. The correct answer is D.

QUESTIONS

Use this diagram to answer questions 342 and 343.

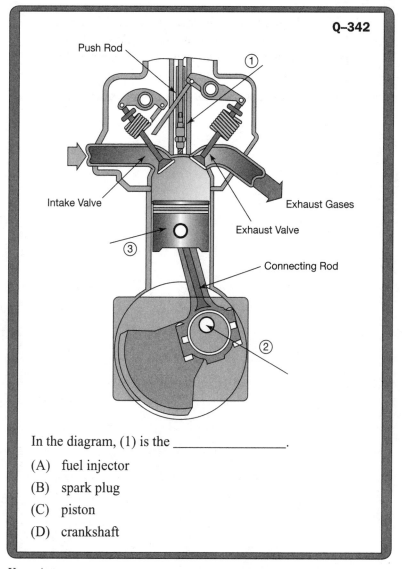

In the diagram, (1) is the _____.

(A) fuel injector

(B) spark plug

(C) piston

(D) crankshaft

Your Answer _____

ANSWERS

A–342

(B) In the diagram, (1) is the spark plug. The crankshaft is (2) and the piston is (3), which you will need to know for the next question. (There is no fuel injector shown in this diagram.) The correct answer is B.

QUESTIONS

Q–343

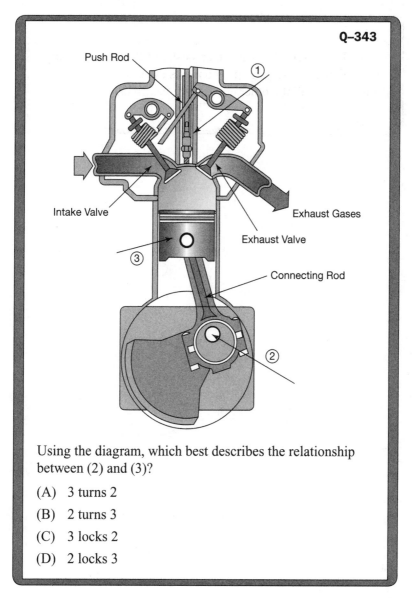

Push Rod

①

Intake Valve

Exhaust Gases

Exhaust Valve

③

Connecting Rod

②

Using the diagram, which best describes the relationship between (2) and (3)?

(A)   3 turns 2

(B)   2 turns 3

(C)   3 locks 2

(D)   2 locks 3

Your Answer _____

ANSWERS

A–343

(A) The piston (3) turns the crankshaft (2); the connecting rod (labeled in the diagram) connects them. The correct answer is A; all the other choices are incorrect.

QUESTIONS

Q–344

Which of the following does NOT apply to automotive systems?

(A) Torque

(B) Combustion

(C) Ventilation

(D) Assimilation

Your Answer _____

Q–345

Three major vehicle-emission pollutants are

(A) hydrocarbons, carbon monoxide, and nitrogen oxides.

(B) hydrocarbons, carbon monoxide, and carbon dioxide.

(C) nitrogen, nitric acid, and nitrous oxide.

(D) chlorofluorcarbons (CFCs), carbon monoxide, and nitrogen.

Your Answer _____

ANSWERS

A–344

(D) Choices A, B, and C are all required for automotive systems to function properly; choice D is a life-science process. Remember that torque refers to turning effort (rotation); combustion (produces heat and light) is necessary to the engine; ventilation is part of the cooling process.

A–345

(A) Three major vehicle-emission pollutants are hydrocarbons, carbon monoxide, and nitrogen oxides. Don't be fooled by the other choices listed! All the choices listed contain pollutants, and each choice contains at least one vehicle-emitted pollutant. The answer must contain three vehicle-emitted pollutants, so the correct answer is A.

QUESTIONS

Q–346

Based on the diagram, which of the following is correct?

(A) 1 is a drum brake and 2 is a disc brake

(B) 1 is a disc brake and 2 is a drum brake

(C) 1 is a spoon brake and 2 is a shoe brake

(D) 1 is a shoe brake and 2 is a spoon brake

Your Answer _____

Q–347

The clutch is used to do which of the following?

(A) Stop the car

(B) Start the car

(C) Increase magnetism

(D) Make it possible to change gears

Your Answer _____

ANSWERS

A–346

(A) According to the diagram's labels, 1 is a drum brake and 2 is a disc brake. There is no such thing as a spoon brake or a shoe brake. A spoon brake is used to adjust drum brakes. Brake shoes are part of both types of brake systems (drum and disc). The correct answer is A.

A–347

(D) The clutch disconnects the engine from the wheels when the car is in neutral or when gears are being shifted. From the choices given as descriptions of the use of the clutch, "makes it possible to change gears" is the correct answer (choice D). None of the other choices is related to the purpose of the clutch.

QUESTIONS

Q–348

Use first gear when

(A) driving at speeds in excess of 35 mph.

(B) driving at speeds in excess of 55 mph.

(C) driving at extremely high speeds to avoid spinning out of control.

(D) starting the engine from a standstill.

Your Answer _____

Q–349

A(n) _____ is used to test battery electrolyte specific gravity.

(A) ammeter

(B) hydrometer

(C) ohmmeter

(D) potentiometer

Your Answer _____

ANSWERS

A–348

(D) First gear is used when starting the engine from a standstill. Once the speed starts to climb, the car needs to be shifted to second and then higher gears, depending upon the actual speed; this rules out choices A, B, and C. The correct answer is D.

A–349

(B) Ammeters measure electrical current; ohmmeters measure ohms; potentiometers are variable resistors; hydrometers are used to test battery electrolyte specific gravity. Again, definitions do need to be memorized, but if you know that ohmmeters and potentiometers measure resistance, you can rule them both out and narrow down the guessing to ammeters and hydrometers. The correct answer is B.

QUESTIONS

Q–350

Which of the following is NOT true about drum brakes?

(A) Pistons push brake shoe and lining against rotating drum.

(B) Drum brakes do not require friction material.

(C) The brake fluid used in drum brake systems is hydraulic.

(D) When the driver hits the brake pedal, pressure builds up in the master cylinder and is transmitted through the brake lines.

Your Answer _____

_____

Q–351

Which of the following is about automotive transmissions?

(A) They trade power for speed.

(B) They control engine speed.

(C) They trade speed for power.

(D) Automatic transmissions do not need torque converters.

Your Answer _____

_____

ANSWERS

A–350

(B) Choices A, C, and D all describe the operation of a drum brake system. However, choice B is NOT true: Drum brakes require friction material, which is called the brake lining. The correct answer is B. Read carefully to notice that the question asks which is NOT true, so you know that three out of four choices will offer accurate information.

A–351

(C) The transmission uses gear reduction to increase engine torque (that is, turning force). As torque increases, speed decreases. The only statement among the choices listed that is true about transmissions is that they trade speed for power (choice C).

QUESTIONS

Q–352

The octane rating

(A) measures gasoline's ability to resist engine knock.

(B) correlates to how much the gasoline can be compressed before it ignites spontaneously.

(C) is not related to preventing premature ignition.

(D) A and B, but not C.

Your Answer _____

_____

Q–353

The instrument that measures revolutions per minute (rpm) is called the _____.

(A) odometer

(B) speedometer

(C) tachometer

(D) chronometer

Your Answer _____

_____

ANSWERS

A–352

(D) The octane rating measures gasoline's ability to resist engine knock and also correlates to how much the gasoline can be compressed before it ignites spontaneously. As a result, using the appropriate octane gasoline will prevent premature ignition. Therefore, choices A and B are true about octane ratings, but choice C is not true. The correct answer is D.

A–353

(C) The instrument that measures revolutions per minute (rpm) is called the tachometer (choice C). The odometer measures the number of miles traveled; the speedometer measures the current speed (miles per hour [mph] and kilometers per hour [kmh]); a chronometer is another word for a timepiece of extreme accuracy (this is not an automotive instrument). The correct answer is C.

QUESTIONS

Q–354

If air gets into the hydraulic brake system,

(A) the brake pedal will stick.

(B) nothing will happen because air has no effect on hydraulic brakes.

(C) brake pedal action will be spongy.

(D) braking application will be hard.

Your Answer _____

_____

Q–355

Which of the following instruments is used to check engine crankshaft end play?

(A) Micrometer

(B) Feeler gauge

(C) Flywheel gauge

(D) Plastigage

Your Answer _____

_____

ANSWERS

A–354

(C) Because air is compressible, it will cause a soft (that is, spongy) brake pedal action (choice C). Neither A, B, nor D is true regarding the results of air entering the hydraulic brake system; the correct answer is C.

A–355

(B) The feeler gauge is used to measure the clearance between the crankshaft and the main thrust bearing; this clearance determines the end play of the crankshaft (choice B). Micrometers are used for very small measurements; they can be used to measure crankshaft journal diameter. The plastigage is used to measure crankshaft-bearing oil clearance. Although the flywheel is pushed by the crankshaft, the flywheel gauge is not a specific instrument. The correct answer is B.

QUESTIONS

Q–356

If the transmission ratio is 3.29 to 1 and the differential ratio is 3.85 to 1, then

(A)   the final ratio is 12.67 to 1.

(B)   the final ratio is 1.17 to 1.

(C)   the final ratio is 7.14 to 1.

(D)   the final ratio is 0.56 to 1.

Your Answer _____

Q–357

Planetary gears

(A)   are used in manual transmissions.

(B)   include sun gears and internal gears.

(C)   provide gear reduction and reverse without shifting.

(D)   B and C, but not A.

Your Answer _____

ANSWERS

A-356

(A) The final ratio of a transmission and differential is calculated by multiplying the ratio of the transmission by the ratio of the differential. Substitute the values given in the question: $3.29 \times 3.85 = 12.67$. The final ratio is 12.67 to 1 (choice A). This question requires that you know how to calculate this ratio, so be sure you understand the ratios, formulas, etc., that are related to automotive systems and operation.

A-357

(D) Planetary gears, which are used in automatic transmissions, are gear trains that use a sun gear, internal gear, and three pinion gears. The three members are in constant mesh and provide gear reduction and reverse without shifting. To obtain gear reduction or reverse, one member must be held stationary by a band or clutch assembly. Therefore, choices B and C are true, but A is not true. The correct answer is D.

QUESTIONS

Q–358

The four-cycle engine actually works in a series of strokes. Which of the following lists these four strokes?

(A) Intake stroke, compression stroke, power stroke, exhaust stroke

(B) Intake stroke, combustion stroke, power stroke, exhaust stroke

(C) Ignition stroke, compression stroke, power stroke, exhaust stroke

(D) Intake stroke, combustion stroke, ignition stroke, exhaust stroke

Your Answer _____

Q–359

All the following statements are true of the flywheel EXCEPT

(A) The flywheel must be properly motivated to maintain the momentum that makes it revolve.

(B) The flywheel revolves between pushes from the crankshaft.

(C) The flywheel does not engage unless the vehicle is in fifth gear or traveling at a speed in excess of 80 mph.

(D) The flywheel keeps the engine going.

Your Answer _____

ANSWERS

A–358

(A) The four-cycle engine actually works in this series of strokes: intake stroke, compression stroke, power stroke, and exhaust stroke (choice A). The other choices are listed to confuse you; to get the right answer here, you simply need to know the names of the four strokes that make up the engine cycle. The correct answer is A.

A–359

(C) In all vehicles, the flywheel, once properly motivated, will continue to revolve by means of momentum between pushes from the crankshaft. In short, the flywheel keeps the engine going. However, it is NOT true that the flywheel only engages if the vehicle is in fifth gear or traveling at a speed in excess of 80 mph. Choices A, B, and D are all true about flywheels; choice C is NOT true. Read carefully—the question specifies that all the statements are true of the flywheel EXCEPT . . . , so you know that you must find an answer choice that is NOT TRUE. The correct answer is C.

QUESTIONS

Q–360

The engine cycle is completed by the accelerator, plus which of the following components?

(A) Carburetor

(B) Throttle

(C) Fuel injector

(D) Either A and B, or B and C

Your Answer _____

Q–361

The engine seizes because of

(A) too much antifreeze in the cooling system.

(B) too much oil in the crankcase.

(C) problems with the lubrication system.

(D) problems with the accelerator.

Your Answer _____

ANSWERS

A–360

(D) The engine cycle is completed by the accelerator, the throttle, and either the carburetor or the fuel injector (fuel injectors are used in most cars manufactured after 1990). Therefore, either A and B or B and C are true. The correct answer is D.

A–361

(C) If all the rotating and reciprocating parts ran against metal without a film of oil between them to reduce friction, they would soon heat up and stick—or "seize." To prevent the engine from seizing, there is a reservoir of oil in the crankcase, which is pumped to the bearings and other critical points in the engine. This oil reservoir, pump, and tubing make up the lubrication system. Thus, problems with the lubrication system can cause the engine to seize. Choices A, B, and D would not cause engine seizing. The correct answer is C.

QUESTIONS

Use this diagram to answer questions 362 and 363.

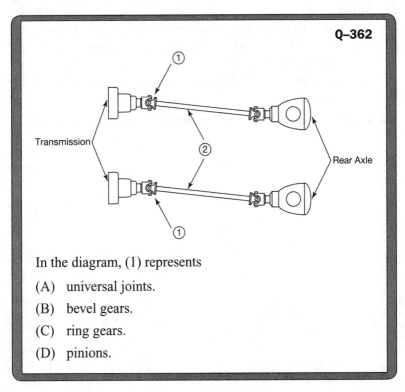

Q–362

Transmission

Rear Axle

In the diagram, (1) represents

(A) universal joints.

(B) bevel gears.

(C) ring gears.

(D) pinions.

Your Answer _____

ANSWERS

A–362

(A) From the labels that do appear, this can be recognized as a rear-wheel-drive transmission because the transmission is connected to the rear axle. In the diagram, (1) represents universal joints; the other choices are not illustrated. The correct answer is A.

QUESTIONS

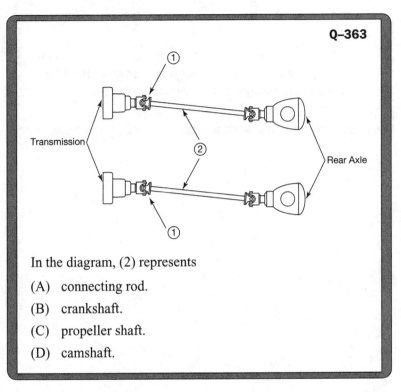

Q–363

In the diagram, (2) represents

(A) connecting rod.

(B) crankshaft.

(C) propeller shaft.

(D) camshaft.

Your Answer _____

_____

ANSWERS

A–363

(C) Again, this represents a rear-wheel-drive transmission. In the diagram, (2) represents the propeller shaft; the other choices are not illustrated. The correct answer is C.

QUESTIONS

Q–364

Which of the following is (are) true about disc brakes?

(A) They are made with two pads and a rotating disc.

(B) The opposing pads with brake lining press against a stationary disc.

(C) Both A and B.

(D) Neither A nor B.

Your Answer _____

Q–365

Which of the following is NOT an example of an automotive emissions-control system?

(A) Combustion inhibitor

(B) Positive-crankcase ventilation

(C) Exhaust-gas-recirculation system

(D) Catalytic converter

Your Answer _____

ANSWERS

A–364

(A) Disc brakes are made with two pads and a rotating disc; the opposing pads with brake lining press against the rotating disc to cause braking. Choice B is incorrect because it specifies "stationary disc," but the disc rotates as stated in choice A. The correct answer is A. Think carefully before choosing "both . . . and" and "neither . . . nor" answers—especially in this instance, where the descriptions of the disc are opposite (that is, rotating and stationary), so you know only one can be correct. As A and B describe a type of disc, the chances of them both being incorrect are slim.

A–365

(A) Without combustion, a car cannot run; that rules out choice A. All the other choices are examples of an automotive emissions-control system. The question asks for which one is NOT, so the correct answer is A.

QUESTIONS

Q–366

This tool is comprised of a handle, a head, a face, a claw, and a wedge.

(A) Hammer

(B) Sledge

(C) Mallet

(D) Wrench

Your Answer _____

Q–367

Which type of saw is used to cut against the grain of the wood?

(A) Ripsaw

(B) Coping saw

(C) Hacksaw

(D) Crosscut saw

Your Answer _____

ANSWERS

A–366

(A) Although sledges, mallets, and hammers are all striking tools with some of the same components, only a hammer has a claw. Wrenches are fastening tools. The correct answer is A.

A–367

(D) Read carefully! The question specifies a saw that cuts against the grain of the wood. A ripsaw cuts with the grain of the wood; a crosscut saw cuts against the grain of the wood, so the correct answer is D. A hacksaw is used to cut metal, and a coping saw is used to cut curved lines or shapes.

QUESTIONS

Q–368

A _____ can measure inside and outside curves, as well as providing very exact, small measurements.

(A) tape rule

(B) caliper

(C) T-square

(D) protractor

Your Answer _____

Q–369

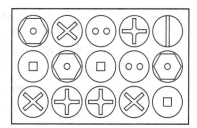

The steel plate shown is held in place by machine screws. According to the diagram, how many different types of screws are being used?

(A) 15

(B) 9

(C) 6

(D) 5

Your Answer _____

ANSWERS

A–368

(B) All choices can be used as measuring tools, but only calipers can perform both functions. Rules and T-squares cannot measure curves of any kind, but sometimes rules are used with calipers to measure diameter. Slide calipers have built-in rules. Protractors are primarily used to measure angles. The correct answer is B.

A–369

(C) The diagram shows a total of 15 screws, but there are only 6 different types. You simply have to look closely and count the different types of machine screws that you see in the image. The correct answer is C.

QUESTIONS

Q–370

Which shape listed below could describe the shape of the head of most bolts?

(A) Oval

(B) Triangle

(C) Octagon

(D) Hexagon

Your Answer _____

Q–371

If you have lay out angles of 45° and 90°, which tool would you use?

(A) T-square

(B) Combination square

(C) Compass

(D) Protractor

Your Answer _____

ANSWERS

A–370

(D) Most bolts have hexagonal heads; the other shapes listed are not common bolt-head shapes. Remember that a hexagon has six sides and six angles—if you know that, then just visualize the bolt head to select the right choice. The correct answer is D.

A–371

(B) If you have lay out angles of 45° and 90°, you would use a combination square, which is specifically used to measure angles of these measurements. A T-square is used to draw lines; a compass is used to draw angles (of all degrees) and circles; a protractor is used to measure angles (of all degrees). The correct answer is B.

QUESTIONS

Q–372

Which of the following is true of welding torches?

(A) They can also be used as cutting torches.

(B) They cannot be used as cutting torches.

(C) They are not safe to use as burning tools or light sources.

(D) A and C, but not B.

Your Answer _____

Q–373

In 28 days, concrete reaches ___ of its strength.

(A) 50 percent

(B) 75 percent

(C) 90 percent

(D) 98 percent

Your Answer _____

ANSWERS

A–372

(D) Welding torches can also be used as cutting torches provided that the proper amount of oxygen is used. They cannot be used as burning tools or light sources. Therefore, A and C are true, but B is not true. The question asks which of the choices are true about welding torches, so the correct answer is D.

A–373

(D) Concrete reaches 98 percent of its strength in 28 days (choice D). No tricks here—you just need to memorize that fact. If you do, this is just another easy one! It is frequently asked on this section of the test.

QUESTIONS

Q–374

Identify which of the following statements is NOT true:

(A) Deciduous trees produce hardwood.

(B) Coniferous trees produce softwood.

(C) Wood must be properly dried before it can be used in furniture or construction.

(D) Because of its hollow structure, wood cannot warp.

Your Answer _____

_____

Q–375

A carpenter who specializes in handcrafted wooden furniture would use a _____ hammer.

(A) planishing

(B) curved-claw

(C) Phillips head

(D) ball-peen

Your Answer _____

_____

ANSWERS

A–374

(D) Deciduous trees (the broad-leafed trees that shed their leaves in winter, such as elms, oaks, maples, etc.) generally produce hardwood; whereas the coniferous trees (needle-bearing evergreens, such as firs, pines, etc.) generally produce softwood. In order to use wood in furniture or construction, it must be properly dried (by air or in a kiln). Although wood does have a hollow structure, it does warp easily, particularly if it gets wet. Therefore, choice D is NOT true. The question specifies identification of the statement that is NOT true, so the correct answer is D. Note that choices C and D are more commonly known; this question is really testing knowledge of which types of trees produce hardwood and softwood (choices A and B).

A–375

(B) For finer work, carpenters prefer to use curved-claw hammers; the claw is used to pull nails. (Straight-claw hammers and sledgehammers are used for rough carpentry work.) Planishing hammers are used to shape or flatten sheet metal; ball-peen hammers are used by machinists; the Phillips head is a type of screwdriver (often just called a Phillips screwdriver), not a hammer. The correct answer is B.

QUESTIONS

Q–376

All of the following are fastening tools EXCEPT

(A) bucking bar.

(B) needle-nose pliers.

(C) Allen wrench.

(D) Phillips screwdriver.

Your Answer _____

ANSWERS

A–376

(A) A bucking bar is used to drive standard rivets; all the other choices listed are fastening tools. Because the question states that all the choices are fastening tools EXCEPT one, the correct answer is A. Pliers are primarily used to fasten and unfasten objects; the jaws of the pliers come together when the handles are squeezed (needle-nose pliers have tapered jaws that enable them to hold small objects and fit in small spaces). Allen wrenches fit hexagonal screw heads, which enables them to fasten/ unfasten hexagonal screws (probably they would have been better named "Allen screwdrivers"). Phillips screwdrivers have a blade that is shaped like a cross, which fits into the cross-shaped Phillips screw. Note that all wrenches and screwdrivers are fastening tools—the difference between them is that screwdrivers only turn screws, but wrenches also turn bolts.

QUESTIONS

Q-377

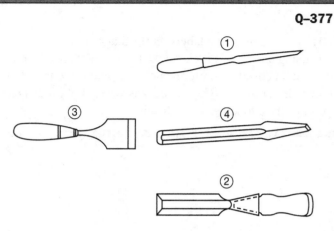

According to the labels on the diagram, which of the following is correct?

(A) 1 is a mortising chisel, and 2 is a socket chisel.

(B) 1 is a socket chisel, and 2 is a mortising chisel.

(C) 3 is a butt chisel, and 4 is a cold chisel.

(D) A and C, but not B.

Your Answer _____

ANSWERS

(D) According to the labels on the diagram, 1 is a mortising chisel, 2 is socket chisel, 3 is a butt chisel, and 4 is a cold chisel. Therefore, choices A and C are true, but choice B is not true. The correct answer is D. With this one, you just have to know your chisels!

QUESTIONS

Q–378

The blade of a coping saw

(A) is placed in the saw so it cuts with the wood grain.

(B) is placed in the saw so it cuts against the wood grain.

(C) is placed in the saw with the teeth pointing toward the handle.

(D) is placed in the saw with the teeth pointing upward.

Your Answer _____

_____

Q–379

This tool will break easily when twisted.

(A) Yardstick

(B) Folding rule

(C) Caliper

(D) Trowel

Your Answer _____

_____

ANSWERS

A–378

(C) The blade of a coping saw is placed in the saw with the teeth facing—or pointing toward—the handle; you cut with a coping saw on the downward stroke, and you need a special type of vise to hold the material to be cut. Coping saws are used to cut curves or any type of line that is not straight. A ripsaw cuts with the grain of the wood; a crosscut saw cuts against it. The correct answer is C.

A–379

(B) The folding rule is infamous for breaking easily when twisted, even slightly. The other tools are not easily broken—or easily twisted, for that matter. The correct answer is B, and it's a simple test of your knowledge of folding rules.

QUESTIONS

Q-380

A mitre box is used to

(A) hold nails.

(B) plane extremely coarse wood.

(C) mount back saws.

(D) shape concrete.

Your Answer _____

_____

Q-381

Overworking concrete means

(A) smoothing it perfectly so that no bubbles remain.

(B) creating depressions in the middle of the slab.

(C) weakening the core of the slab.

(D) causing it to separate and create a less durable surface.

Your Answer _____

_____

ANSWERS

A–380

(C) Mitre boxes are exclusively used to mount back saws (the ones with the metal band across the top) in order to cut angles as needed or provided by the type of mitre box used. The other choices are not related to mitre boxes in any way. The correct answer is C.

A–381

(D) If you overwork concrete, all the water will come to the surface, along with the cement. The heavier particles then settle farther down into the slab, resulting in separation and a less durable surface when the concrete dries. Choices A, B, and C do not describe the results of overworking concrete, but choice D does, so it is the correct answer.

QUESTIONS

Q–382

If you want to mark, cut, and smooth wood, which of the following basic tools would you use?

(A) Chisel, saw, and file

(B) Scratch awl, saw, and plane

(C) Screwdriver, shears, and file

(D) Caliper, saw, and plane

Your Answer _____

Q–383

You would use a _____ to hold material that you need to drill, saw, or glue.

(A) weight

(B) plane

(C) wrench

(D) vise

Your Answer _____

ANSWERS

A–382

(B) The basic tools you would use to mark, cut, and smooth wood are scratch awls, saws, and planes, respectively. The specific type you used would depend upon the project. Although some of the choices contain the proper tool for one job, only one lists all three in correct order: choice B, the correct answer.

A–383

(D) You would use a vise to hold material that you need to drill, saw, or glue. You might put a weight on top of loose papers to keep them from blowing off your workbench on a breezy day when the door or window is open. You would use a plane to smooth wood; there are various types of wrenches, all of which are used as fasteners. The correct answer is D.

QUESTIONS

Q-384

Which of the metals listed below can be made thinner than a coat of paint?

(A) Aluminum

(B) Silver

(C) Gold

(D) Copper

Your Answer _____

Q-385

The most efficient and safest way to make a hole in sheet metal is to

(A) cut it.

(B) burn it.

(C) drill it.

(D) punch it.

Your Answer _____

449

ANSWERS

A-384

(C) Gold can be hammered into leaves so thin that
only a special type of brush can pick them up—this is
often referred to as "gold leaf" and is used in fine art
and architecture (for example, the domes of state capitol
buildings and certain churches). The gold leaf is placed
on the surface to be covered and then burnished (rubbed)
with a smooth piece of metal until it sticks to the intended
surface. The other metals listed cannot be hammered into
leaves (foil) that thin. The correct answer is C.

A-385

(D) The most efficient and safest way to make a hole in
sheet metal is by punching it. Cutting and burning are not
efficient (or necessarily safe); drilling can be extremely
dangerous because, if the sheet metal is not properly
secured, the drill bit can catch and spin—the drill-bit
operator could easily be cut if he/she does not get out
of the way of the spinning bit fast enough. The correct
answer is D.

QUESTIONS

Q–386

Which of the following is NOT true about steel?

(A) It is an alloy of iron.

(B) It is not as strong as iron.

(C) It is made with carbon.

(D) It does not rust.

Your Answer _____

Q–387

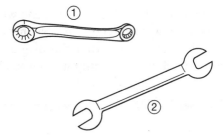

According to the diagram

(A) 1 is a box end wrench, and 2 is an open end wrench.

(B) 1 is an open end wrench, and 2 is a box end wrench.

(C) 1 is a ratchet, and 2 is an open end wrench.

(D) 1 is a ratchet, and 2 is an adjustable wrench.

Your Answer _____

ANSWERS

A–386

(B)   Steel is an alloy of iron; as an alloy, it has added strength. It is made with carbon (and some types of steel have other metals in addition, for example, chromium steel), and it does not rust. Choices A, C, and D are true; choice B is not true. The question asks which statement is NOT true about steel, so the correct answer is B.

A–387

(A)   According to the diagram, 1 is a box end wrench, and 2 is an open end wrench (choice A). Neither a ratchet nor an adjustable wrench is shown in this diagram. This question tests your ability to identify wrenches. The correct answer is A.

QUESTIONS

Q–388

Bolting and riveting

(A) provide a temporary connection between two metals.

(B) provide a less permanent connection between metals than welding provides.

(C) are the same as soldering.

(D) A and B, but not C.

Your Answer _____

Q–389

Which type of saw is used to cut metal?

(A) Coping saw

(B) Crosscut saw

(C) Hacksaw

(D) Ripsaw

Your Answer _____

ANSWERS

A–388

(D) Bolting and riveting provide a temporary connection between two metals; welding provides a permanent connection between metals; soldering connects using a material called solder, but it is not the same as bolting and riveting. Therefore, choices A and B are correct, but choice C is incorrect. The correct answer is D.

A–389

(C) A hacksaw is used to cut metal (choice C). Coping saws are used to cut curves or any type of line that is not straight; crosscut saws cut against the wood grain; and ripsaws cut with it. The correct answer is C.

QUESTIONS

Q–390

All the following statements are true of concrete EXCEPT

(A) it is a mixture of cement, sand, and water.

(B) the cement and water form a paste that binds the other materials together as the concrete hardens.

(C) hardened concrete is very strong and is also both fireproof and waterproof.

(D) gravel cannot be included in the concrete mix.

Your Answer _____

ANSWERS

A–390

(D) Concrete is a mixture of cement, sand, and water; the cement and water form a paste that binds the other materials together as the concrete hardens. Hardened concrete is very strong and is also both fireproof and waterproof. Gravel can be included in the concrete mix, but all the concrete ingredients must be added in the proper proportions and mixed to form the correct consistency (concrete mixes are also available; all you do is add the water as directed). Therefore, choices A, B, and C all are true, but choice D is not true. The question specifies that all the statements are true EXCEPT one, so the correct answer is D.

QUESTIONS

Q–391

A first-class lever has a resistance arm of 3' and an effort arm of 6'. What is its mechanical advantage?

(A) 9

(B) 3

(C) 2

(D) 18

Your Answer _____

Q–392

Air weighs approximately 15 psi (pounds per square inch). What is the amount of pressure (force) that is exerted on a banquet table with a surface area of 48 inches?

(A) 720 pounds

(B) 0.3125 pound

(C) 5/16 pound

(D) 63 pounds

Your Answer _____

ANSWERS

A–391

(C) The formula for calculating mechanical advantage (MA) is: length of effort arm divided by length of resistance arm; MA = 6 ÷ 3; MA = 2. The other choices use addition, subtraction, and multiplication as incorrect expressions of the formula. The correct answer is C.

A–392

(A) Power equals force divided by area in square inches ($P = F \div A$), which can also be expressed as $F = A \times P$. Substituting the numbers stated in the question, $F = 15 \times 48$; $F = 720$, (choice A). Choices B and C use this formula incorrectly, dividing 15 by 48, and then expressing the answer in decimal and fractional forms, respectively. Choice D also uses this formula incorrectly, adding 15 and 48.

QUESTIONS

Q–393

After it hits the wall, a handball "bounces" back to the player because of the force known as

(A) friction.

(B) gravity.

(C) magnetism.

(D) recoil.

Your Answer _____

Q–394

Select the choice below that best describes the difference between mass and weight:

(A) Mass and weight are equivalent.

(B) Mass is relative, based on gravity; weight can be changed by buoyancy.

(C) Mass depends on velocity, but weight always remains constant.

(D) Mass always remains constant, but weight varies, depending on altitude.

Your Answer _____

ANSWERS

A–393

(D) All the choices listed are examples of force. Friction is resistance to motion against a touched surface. Gravity is the force that draws objects toward the earth. Magnetism attracts iron or steel. Recoil is the property of "kicking," or "bouncing," back after release. The correct answer is (D).

A–394

(D) Of the choices listed, the best description of the difference between mass and weight is that mass always remains constant, but weight varies, depending on altitude (choice D). Mass remains constant no matter where an object is, but the weight of an object will vary, depending on its distance from the gravitational pull of the earth. Only choice D fits this definition; all the other choices are incorrect.

QUESTIONS

Q–395

Which of the following is false?

(A) Unlike poles attract.

(B) Like poles repel.

(C) North attracts north.

(D) South attracts north.

Your Answer _____

Q–396

Torque can be defined as

(A) turning effort.

(B) number of cylinders.

(C) driveshaft.

(D) ratio of driveshaft to rear axle.

Your Answer _____

ANSWERS

A–395

(C) Unlike poles attract; like poles repel. Thus, choices A, B, and D are all true. However, north cannot attract north (because like poles repel, they do not attract). North attracts north is false, so the correct answer is C. Be sure to read carefully—the question asks which statement is false.

A–396

(A) Torque can be defined as turning effort (choice A). Choice B (number of cylinders) is not relevant to the question. As for choices C and D, the differential (that is, ratio) that connects the driveshaft to the rear axle increases engine torque through gear reduction because the driveshaft turns faster than the rear axles; but this is an instance of torque, not a definition of it. The correct answer is A.

QUESTIONS

Q–397

Pliers would be an example of a

(A) pivot.

(B) first-class lever.

(C) second-class lever.

(D) third-class lever.

Your Answer _____

Use the diagram to answer questions 398 and 399.

Q–398

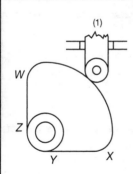

In the diagram shown, (1) is an example of a type of

(A) gear.

(B) follower.

(C) pulley.

(D) cam.

Your Answer _____

ANSWERS

A-397

(B) A lever is a rigid bar that is pivoted at some point.
A pivot, therefore, is part of a lever, ruling out choice A. In a
first-class lever, the pivot is between the effort and the load,
as with pliers. A second-class lever has the pivot at one end,
the effort at the other end, and the load in between—as with a
wheelbarrow. In a third-class lever, the effort is in the middle
(between the pivot and the load), as with ice tongs. Therefore,
pliers would be an example of a first-class lever (choice B).
Rules about levers and other simple machines do just need
to be memorized. Don't be fooled by the inclusion of pivot,
which is associated with levers, but is not a type of lever itself.

A-398

(B) In the diagram shown, (1) is an example of a type
of follower. It does not illustrate any of the other choices
shown. The correct answer is B.

QUESTIONS

Q–399

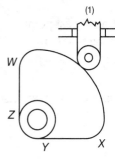

In the diagram shown, (1) will be at its lowest point between points _____.

(A) W and Z

(B) X and Y

(C) W and X

(D) Y and Z

Your Answer _____

Q–400

A magnetic clutch works by

(A) friction.

(B) hydraulics.

(C) induction.

(D) pneumatics.

Your Answer _____

ANSWERS

A–399

(D) In the diagram shown, (1) will be at its lowest point between points Y and Z (choice D). Knowing that (1) is a follower will help you correctly answer this second question related to the same diagram.

A–400

(C) The terms *magnetic clutch* and *induction clutch* are used interchangeably; therefore, a magnetic clutch works by induction (choice C). If you were asked what an induction clutch works by, the answer would be magnetism. All the other choices are incorrect.

QUESTIONS

Q–401

Which of the following is (are) an example(s) of force?

(A) Friction

(B) Gravity

(C) Buoyancy

(D) All of the above

Your Answer _____

Q–402

If an object is in equilibrium

(A) it must be completely at rest.

(B) it is at rest or moving at a constant speed in a straight line.

(C) the total force acting on it in any direction is exactly equal in magnitude to the force in the opposite direction.

(D) B and C, but not A.

Your Answer _____

ANSWERS

A–401

(D) Friction, gravity, and buoyancy are all examples of force (choice D). Other forces include lift, elastic recoil, magnetism, and electric force. Here is another question that tests knowledge of basic definitions. Memorize those principles!

A–402

(D) If an object is in equilibrium, it is at rest or moving at a constant speed in a straight line AND the total force acting on it in any direction is exactly equal in magnitude to the force in the opposite direction. It is not true that an object in equilibrium must be completely at rest. Therefore, choices B and C are true of an object in equilibrium, but choice A is not. The correct answer is D. Again, being clear about these principles is key to test success.

QUESTIONS

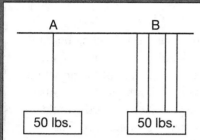

Q-403

A   B

50 lbs. 50 lbs.

Two 50-lb. boards are attached to a beam using cords, as illustrated above. Which one of the following statements is true?

(A) All cords are under the same tension because gravity acts on them equally.

(B) The cord holding board A is under ¼ the tension of the cords holding board B.

(C) The cords holding board B are under ¼ the tension of the cord holding board A.

(D) The cords holding board B are under ⅛ the tension of the cord holding board A.

Your Answer _____

_____

ANSWERS

A–403

(C) Given the illustration, the four cords holding board B are under ¼ the tension of the single cord holding board A. This is a simple test of your understanding of the principle of tension. If you consider the question logically, because the objects are of the same weight, the four cords would have to be under less tension than the single cord. The correct answer is C; all the other choices are incorrect.

QUESTIONS

Q–404

An airplane is in equilibrium under four balanced forces: lift, weight, drag and _____.

(A) thrust

(B) camber

(C) recoil

(D) magnetism

Your Answer _____

ANSWERS

A–404

(A) An airplane is in equilibrium under four balanced forces: lift, weight, drag, and thrust (choice A). Lift and weight are the forces in balance vertically; drag and thrust are the forces in balance horizontally. Camber is used to describe a curved surface; it is not a type of force. Elastic recoil is a type of force related to solids, but it has nothing to do with airplanes in equilibrium. Magnetism is also a force, but again, not related to airplane equilibrium. The correct answer is A.

QUESTIONS

Q–405

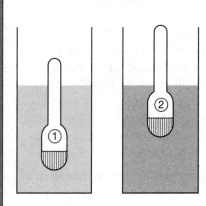

In the diagram shown, floats 1 and 2 measure the specific gravity of two different liquids. Which float indicates the liquid with the lowest specific gravity?

(A) 1

(B) 2

(C) Neither 1 nor 2

(D) 1 and 2 have the same specific gravity

Your Answer _____

_____

ANSWERS

A–405

(A) Float 1 indicates the liquid with the lowest specific gravity (choice A). Hydrometers use floats to measure specific gravity, which is the weight of a liquid compared to the weight of water. The liquid with the lowest specific gravity will remain lower in the glass tube; conversely, the liquid with the highest specific gravity will rise higher in the tube. Because the floats are in different positions, you can rule out choices C and D. The correct answer is A.

QUESTIONS

Q–406

In mechanical devices _____ are used to change torque.

(A) winches

(B) gears

(C) cranks

(D) levers

Your Answer _____

Q–407

Springs that are used in machines are most often made of

(A) nylon fiber.

(B) plastic.

(C) steel.

(D) industrial diamonds.

Your Answer _____

ANSWERS

A–406

(B) In mechanical devices, gears are used to change torque (turning effort). Winches, cranks, and levers are all examples of simple machines, but they are not used specifically to change torque; gears are. The correct answer is B.

A–407

(C) Springs that are used in machines are most often made of steel; sometimes they are made of brass or other metal alloys, but never of the other choices listed here. The correct answer is C.

QUESTIONS

Q–408

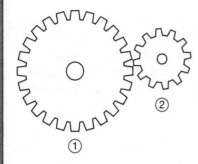

In the diagram, if gear 1 has 28 teeth and gear 2 has 16 teeth, how many revolutions does gear 2 make for every 12 revolutions that gear 1 makes?

(A) 16

(B) 12

(C) 21

(D) 28

Your Answer _____

ANSWERS

A–408

(C) To determine the answer, multiply the number of teeth in gear 1 (*D*) by the number of revolutions it makes (*R*). Then, divide that number by the number of teeth in gear 2 (*d*) to determine the number of revolutions gear 2 makes (*r*). The gears are proportional, so this formula will give the ratio of teeth to revolutions:

$r = DR/d$

$r = 28 \times 12/16$

$r = 336/16$

$r = 21$ (choice C)

QUESTIONS

Q–409

A plastic hanger, a wooden spatula, a rubber hose, and a silver spoon all are the same temperature. Which of them feels the coldest?

(A)   Rubber hose

(B)   Silver spoon

(C)   Plastic hanger

(D)   Wooden spatula

Your Answer _____

_____

ANSWERS

A–409

(B) If a plastic hanger, a wooden spatula, a rubber hose, and a silver spoon are all the same temperature, the silver spoon will feel the coldest (choice B). This is because metal is the best conductor of all of the materials listed.

QUESTIONS

Q–410

The pressure gauge shown indicates a reading of

(A) 17.0.

(B) 27.0.

(C) 25.2.

(D) 20.3.

Your Answer _____

ANSWERS

A–410

(B) The pressure gauge shown indicates a reading of 27.0 (choice B). This question tests ability to read measurement markings. Remember, sometimes they are just easy questions—if you feel you know the answer to a seemingly simple question, as long as you read and view carefully, don't overthink.

QUESTIONS

Q–411

Which of the following is used to measure extremely high resistance?

(A) Ammeter

(B) Ohmmeter

(C) Potentiometer

(D) Megger

Your Answer _____

Q–412

Two strips of metal—one brass, one iron—that are welded or riveted together would form a

(A) thermometer.

(B) rheometer.

(C) thermostat.

(D) rheostat.

Your Answer _____

ANSWERS

A–411

(D) Ammeters measure electrical current; ohmmeters measure ohms; potentiometers are variable resistors. The meter used to measure extremely high resistance is called a megger (choice D). This question is intended to confuse you, because if you know that ohmmeters and potentiometers are both related to resistance, you might consider that one of them could be a valid answer. However, the key part of this question is "extremely high resistance." The *megger* is so named because the units of measurement it gives will be in the millions—*megs*—because they are extremely high.

A–412

(C) A thermometer is usually some type of calibrated, fine glass tube with a liquid (e.g., mercury) sealed inside it—the liquid rises and falls with changes in temperature. A rheometer measures the flow of viscous substances; a rheostat regulates current by means of variable resistances. Two strips of metal—one brass, one iron—that are welded or riveted together would form a thermostat, a device that moves a switch to turn a heating or cooling device on or off as the temperature makes these metals expand or contract. The correct answer is C.

QUESTIONS

Q–413

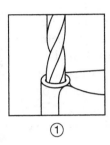 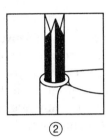

① ②

Which of the following would describe what is shown in this diagram?

(A) The hole is being drilled in 1 and tapped in 2.

(B) The hole is being tapped in 1 and drilled in 2.

(C) The hole is being drilled in 1 and plugged in 2.

(D) The hole is being plugged in 1 and tapped in 2.

Your Answer _____

Q–414

Which of the following would prevent condensation from forming on cold-water pipes?

(A) Keeping the long sections of pipe vertical.

(B) Insulating the pipes.

(C) Maintaining the cold water at a temperature of 32°F.

(D) Ensuring that no air enters the cold-water pipes.

Your Answer _____

ANSWERS

A–413

(A) The diagram illustrates a hole that is being drilled in 1 and tapped in 2 (choice A). It is relatively easy to determine that 1 shows a drill, which rules out choices B and D. This question is really designed to see if you know that a tap is a tool used to make threads in the drilled hole. If you know that, you will automatically rule out choice C. Even if you don't know that, a plug would be solid. The correct answer is A.

A–414

(B) Of the choices listed, only insulating the pipes would prevent condensation from forming on them (choice B). All the other choices are incorrect.

QUESTIONS

Q–415

Which is the value of atmospheric pressure under normal conditions?

(A) 7.4 psi

(B) 10.7 psi

(C) 14.7 psi

(D) 22.1 psi

Your Answer _____

Q–416

A micrometer measures

(A) minuscule changes in temperature.

(B) objects too small to be seen by the human eye without a visual aid.

(C) extremely small variations in psi.

(D) thicknesses to a few thousandths of an inch.

Your Answer _____

ANSWERS

A–415

(C) Under normal conditions, atmospheric pressure is 14.7 psi (pounds per square inch). None of the other choices lists accurate answers; this is another instance where you just have to memorize the value. The correct answer is C.

A–416

(D) A micrometer measures small, but not invisible, objects, so thicknesses to a few thousandths of an inch would be measured by a micrometer (choice D). The other choices are not measured by micrometers, but note that the descriptions of smallness are contextual clues, so if you happen to get another question about micrometers with choices describing it as other than small, you can rule them out.

QUESTIONS

Use the diagram to answer questions 417 and 418.

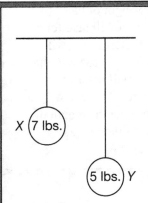

Q–417

In the diagram shown, which pendulum would take less time to make a complete swing?

(A) X

(B) Y

(C) X and Y would take the same amount of time to make a complete swing

(D) Gravity would need to be specified in order to determine which—X or Y—would make a complete swing in less time

Your Answer _____

_____

ANSWERS

A–417

(A) The length of the string, not the weight of the pendulum, is what determines how long it will take for a complete swing. In other words, the shortest string will swing fastest. You can rule out choice C by reasoning that either the weight or the length of string will determine which swings faster. Choice D is incorrect because weight (determined by gravity) does not determine the length of the swing. Pendulum X would take less time to make a complete swing than pendulum Y (choice A).

QUESTIONS

Q-418

In the diagram shown, if the string holding pendulum Y were cut to be the same length as the string holding pendulum X, which of the following would happen?

(A) X would still make a complete swing in less time.

(B) Y would make a complete swing in less time than X.

(C) X and Y would take the same amount of time to make a complete swing.

(D) X and Y will no longer be able to swing hanging next to each other because their strings are the same length.

Your Answer _____

_____

ANSWERS

A–418

(C)   As already explained above, the length of the string, not the weight, determines how long a swing will take. If the strings are the same length, X and Y will take the same amount of time to make a complete swing (choice C). You need to understand this principle to get the right answer, but you can automatically rule out choice D; hanging next to each other from strings of the same length would not prevent X and Y from swinging.

QUESTIONS

Q–419

Which of the following metals will expand the least when heated?

(A) Aluminum

(B) Tungsten

(C) Iron

(D) Steel

Your Answer _____

Q–420

The phenomenon that causes oil to rise in lamp wicks, melted wax to rise in candle wicks, and water to rise in a narrow tube is called

(A) lift.

(B) osmosis.

(C) wicking.

(D) capillarity.

Your Answer _____

ANSWERS

A–419

(B) All metals expand when heated. Of the ones listed here, tungsten expands the least when heated (choice B). For this reason, it is often used as an incandescent lamp filament. Of the choices listed, aluminum expands the most when heated. The correct answer is B.

A–420

(D) Lift is a type of force; osmosis is the gradual penetration of a shell or membrane; wicking is a material's ability to absorb or drain fluid (like the wick of candle or oil lamp). *Capillarity* (also called capillary action) is the term used for the phenomenon that causes oil to rise in lamp wicks, melted wax to rise in candle wicks, and water to rise in a narrow tube (choice D). Note that because wicks are specified in the question, the likelihood of wicking being a valid answer is slim. The correct answer is D.

QUESTIONS

Q–421

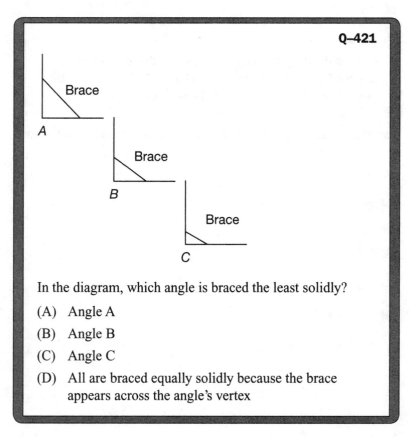

In the diagram, which angle is braced the least solidly?

(A)   Angle A

(B)   Angle B

(C)   Angle C

(D)   All are braced equally solidly because the brace appears across the angle's vertex

Your Answer _____

ANSWERS

A–421

(C) In the diagram, angle C is braced the least solidly (choice C). Do not be fooled by choice D; the vertex is the only place where an angle can be braced.

QUESTIONS

Q–422

A high-tech ceramic tool, a silver tool, and a steel tool are all placed in water at 100°C so that they can be cleaned. Which of the tools will get the hottest?

(A) Steel

(B) Silver

(C) High-tech ceramic

(D) All three tools will get equally hot because the water is the same temperature

Your Answer _____

Q–423

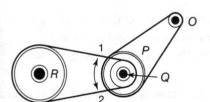

The diagram shown illustrates what type of machine?

(A) Pulley

(B) Winch

(C) Vise

(D) Gear

Your Answer _____

ANSWERS

A–422

(B) Of the materials listed, silver is the best conductor, so it will get the hottest. The correct answer is B. (Note that even if all are in water of the same temperature, the best conductor still gets the hottest.)

A–423

(A) The diagram shown illustrates a pulley connected by belts. All the other choices are also examples of simple machines, but this diagram does not look like any of them. The correct answer is A.

QUESTIONS

Q–424

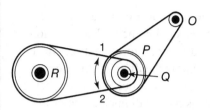

In the diagram shown, O is the driver and turns in direction 1. Which will turn the fastest?

(A) R

(B) P

(C) Q

(D) O

Your Answer _____

Q–425

Which playground fixture is an example of a lever?

(A) Swing

(B) Glider

(C) Sandbox shovel

(D) Seesaw

Your Answer _____

ANSWERS

A–424

(D)   As you know from the first question related to this diagram, this is a pulley connected by belts. The question tells us that pulley O is the driver and turns in direction 1; however, you don't need to know the direction in order to answer the question. When a series of pulleys is connected by belts, the pulley with the smallest diameter rotates at the fastest speed; conversely, the pulley with the largest diameter rotates at the slowest speed. Pulley O has the smallest diameter, so it would turn the fastest (choice D). Use your knowledge! Don't be fooled into thinking that because O is named in the question it can't be the correct answer—it most definitely *is* correct.

A–425

(D)   A seesaw is a type of lever; none of the other choices listed are levers. Specifically, a seesaw is a first-class lever. Can you figure out why? As with all first-class levers, the pivot (that is, fulcrum) is between the effort and the load. Note that seesaws are commonly used as examples of levers on the test.

QUESTIONS

Directions:

This test concerns your ability to mentally picture items in three dimensions. Each question is composed of five separate drawings. The problem is presented in the first drawing and the remaining four drawings are possible solutions. Choose the best answer to each question and then darken the oval on your answer sheet.

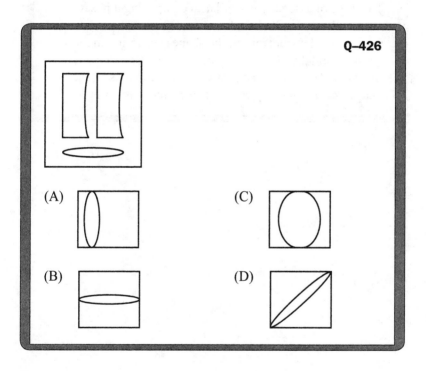

Q–426

(A)   (C)

(B)   (D)

Your Answer _____

_____

ANSWERS

A–426

(B)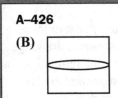

This type of assembly is similar to completing a jigsaw puzzle. When you look at the answer choices, be sure to pick one that contains all the shapes appearing in the question and that they all are the right size and shape. In this instance, only one answer choice contains all the images shown in the question. The correct answer is B.

QUESTIONS

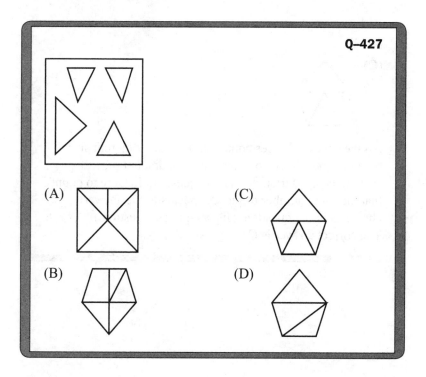

Q–427

(A)

(B)

(C)

(D)

Your Answer _____

ANSWERS

A–427

(C)

All the answer choices contain triangles of different sizes, but only one choice contains the same amount of, and accurately sized triangles as, the question. Be sure to count that the same number of pieces appears in the answer choice as in the question. (Jigsaw-puzzle question.)
The correct answer is C.

QUESTIONS

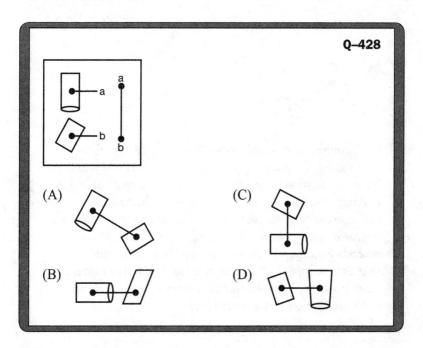

Your Answer _____

_____

ANSWERS

A–428

(A)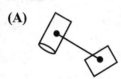

Line-connector assembly is somewhat more complicated than the jigsaw-puzzle assembly problems. The key to these types of questions is: Checking the placement of the points, making sure that the line axis is in the right position, and also making sure the answer choice you pick is not a mirror image—that this is the biggest pitfall in this type of assembly problem! Choices A and C both show the same shapes that appear in the question, as well as the correct point position, but only choice A shows the correct line position. The correct answer is A.

QUESTIONS

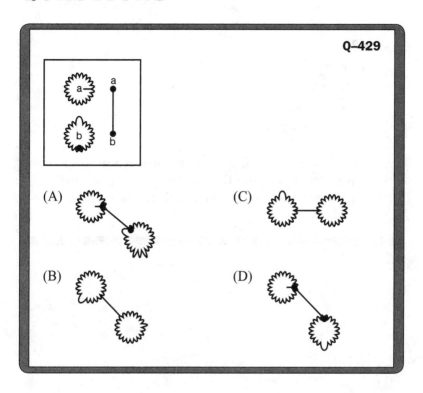

Your Answer _____

ANSWERS

A–429

(D)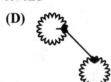

All the choices show the same shapes that appear in the question, but only choice D shows the correct point and line positions. (Line-connector question.) The correct answer is D.

QUESTIONS

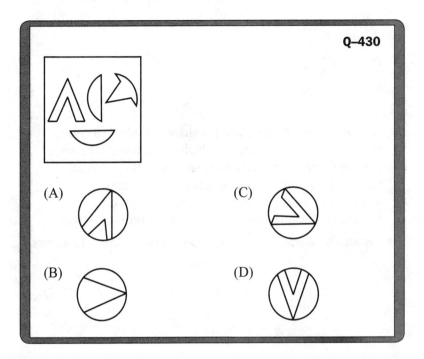

Q–430

(A)

(C)

(B)

(D)

Your Answer _____

_____

ANSWERS

A–430

(C)

All the answer choices show the shapes fitted into a circle, so you need to check and see which one contains the same amount of, and accurately sized shapes as, the question. Only C does—the odd shape between the V shape is the key piece to look for when choosing your answer! (Jigsaw-puzzle question.) The correct answer is C.

QUESTIONS

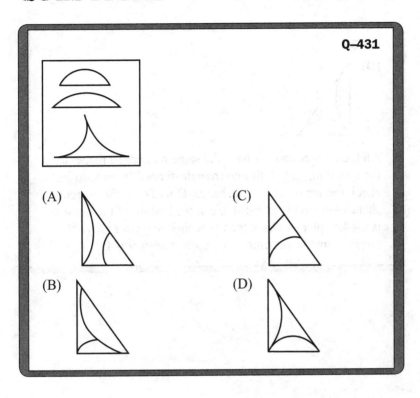

Q–431

(A)

(B)

(C)

(D)

Your Answer _____

ANSWERS

A–431

(D)

All the answer choices have the same number of pieces as the question, and all fit into triangle-shaped frames, so just check for accurately sized shapes. Only D has the correct shapes—the odd curved shape at the bottom of the question is the key piece to look for when choosing your answer! (Jigsaw-puzzle question.) The correct answer is D.

QUESTIONS

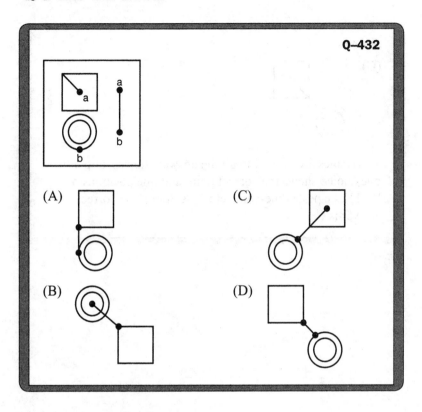

Q-432

(A)

(C)

(B)

(D)

Your Answer _____

ANSWERS

A–432

(C)

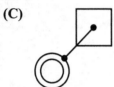

The shapes are correct in all the answer choices, but only one choice shows the correct point and line positions on BOTH shapes. (Line-connector question.) The correct answer is C.

QUESTIONS

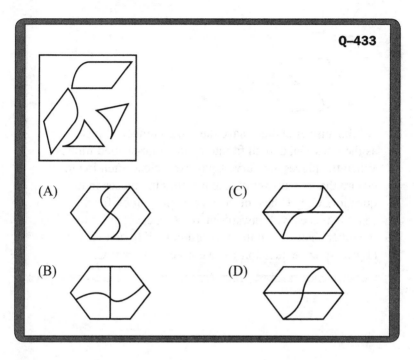

Q–433

(A)

(C)

(B)

(D)

Your Answer _____

515

ANSWERS

(C)

All the answer choices have the same number of pieces as the question, and all fit into rectangular-shaped frames. When the pieces are curved, pay extra close attention to ensure that the answer choice matches the pieces in the question. Only C has the correct shapes—look for the triangle pieces with inward-curved (concave) sides to fit the other shapes with the outward-curved (convex) sides. (Jigsaw-puzzle question.) The correct answer is C.

QUESTIONS

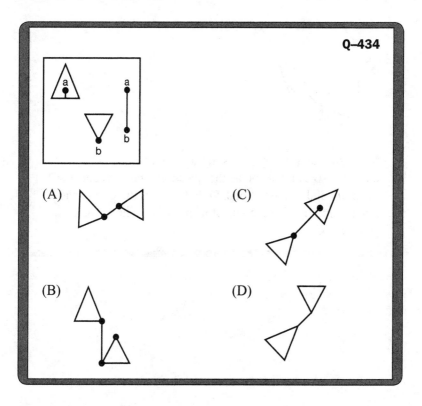

Q-434

(A)

(B)

(C)

(D)

Your Answer _____

ANSWERS

A–434

(C)

Make sure that the triangles in the answer choice are of the same size and shape as the question, and then check the point and line positions. Only C shows the points and line accurately. (Line-connector question.) The correct answer is C.

QUESTIONS

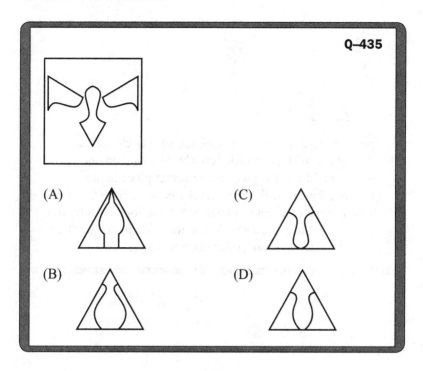

Q–435

Your Answer _____

_____

ANSWERS

A–435

(C)

This is more difficult because all the answer choices are relatively similar. Narrow it down by focusing on one piece—the best is the piece in the center piece in the question, the one with the triangular bottom. Both C and D show a shape that looks similar, but if you look closely, you can see that the curved part of it is too wide in choice D. (Jigsaw-puzzle question.) The correct answer is C.

QUESTIONS

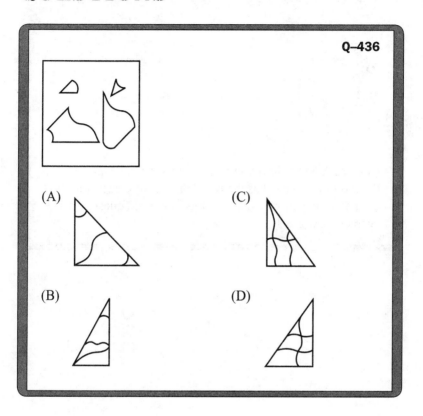

Q–436

(A)

(C)

(B)

(D)

Your Answer _____

ANSWERS

A–436

(D)

Choices A and B have too many pieces, so you can rule them out. Choice C has the right number of pieces, but they are not all the correct shapes. (Jigsaw-puzzle question.) The correct answer is D.

QUESTIONS

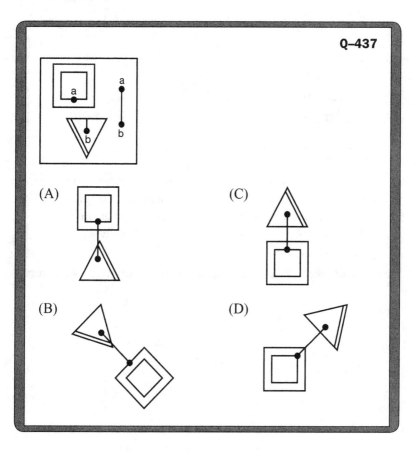

Q–437

Your Answer _____

ANSWERS

A–437

(C)

The shapes are correct in all the answer choices, so you just need to check the point and line positions. Only one answer choice shows the correct point and line positions without flipping the axis. (Line-connector question.) The correct answer is C.

QUESTIONS

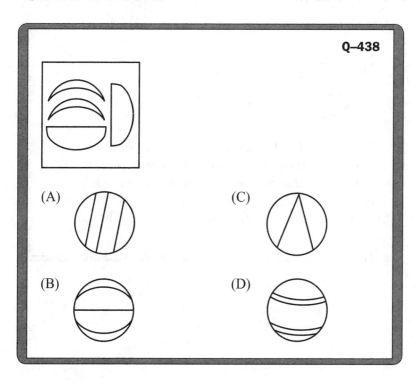

Q–438

(A)

(C)

(B)

(D)

Your Answer _____

ANSWERS

A–438

(B)

Choices C and D do not have the right number of pieces, so you can rule them out. Choice A has the right number of pieces, but they are not all the correct shapes. Only one choice has the correct number of pieces, all of which match the question. (Jigsaw-puzzle question.) The correct answer is B.

QUESTIONS

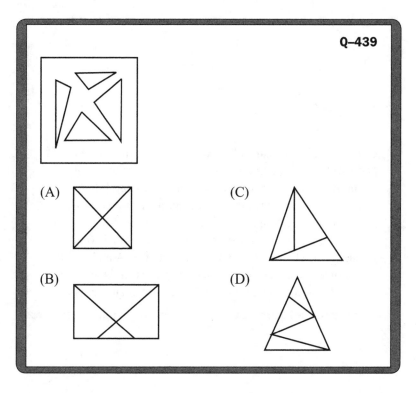

Q–439

(A)

(B)

(C)

(D)

Your Answer _____

ANSWERS

A–439

(D)

Check the choices carefully: two have triangular frames
and two have rectangular frames, so you have to count
the number of pieces and check their shapes carefully!
Choice C does not have the correct number of pieces. The
pieces in the question are distinctive and of different size
and shape, so look for an answer that matches that when
checking the shapes. You can rule out choices A and B. Only
one choice has the correct number of pieces AND the correct
shapes. (Jigsaw-puzzle question.) The correct answer is D.

QUESTIONS

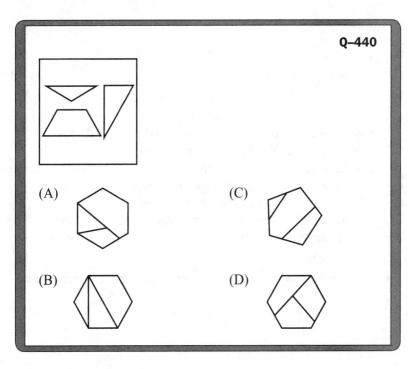

Q–440

(A)

(B)

(C)

(D)

Your Answer _____

529

ANSWERS

A-440

(B)

Again, check the choices carefully—all the frame shapes are not the same. You MUST count the number of pieces and check their shapes carefully! The key piece to look for in the answer choices is the trapezoid (shape in the question that is NOT a triangle). Only one choice has this shape drawn correctly—it is misshapen in choices A and D, and does not appear in C. (Jigsaw-puzzle question.) The correct answer is B.

QUESTIONS

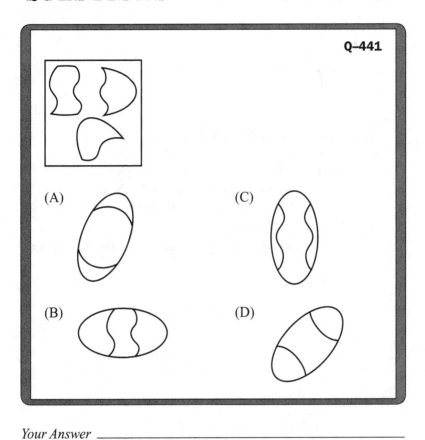

Q–441

(A)

(B)

(C)

(D)

Your Answer _____

ANSWERS

A–441

(B)

When the pieces are curved, pay extra close attention to ensure that the answer choice you select matches the pieces in the question! All the pieces in the question have more than one curve, ruling out choices A and D. Choice C does not match the shapes in the question. (Jigsaw-puzzle question.) The correct answer is B.

QUESTIONS

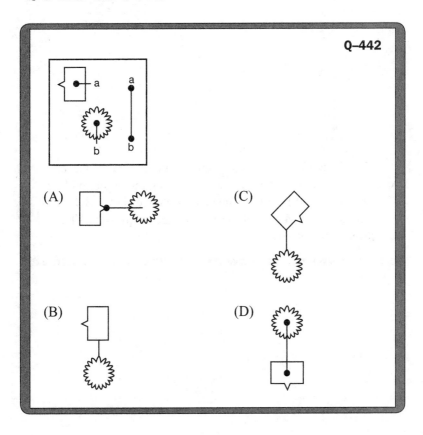

Your Answer _____

ANSWERS

A–442

(D)

First, check the shapes—they are correct in all the answer choices, so that means you need to check the point and line positions carefully. Only one answer choice shows BOTH point positions accurately. (Line-connector question.) The correct answer is D.

QUESTIONS

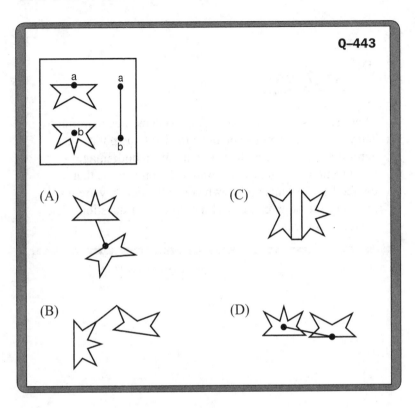

Q–443

Your Answer _____

ANSWERS

A–443

(D)

These shapes are easily confused, so check them carefully. They are all correct, so you need to check the points carefully, too, because they are similar on both images in the question—again, easily confused. You can see that in choice D, the points are shown correctly, but they are not in any of the other choices. (Line-connector question.) The correct answer is D.

QUESTIONS

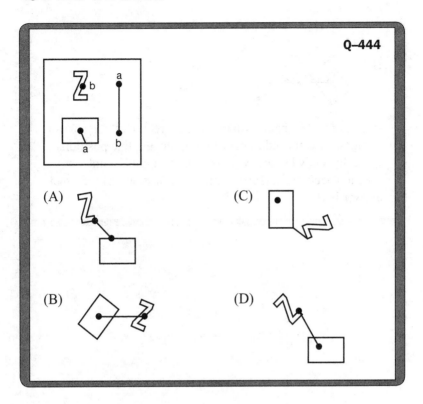

Your Answer _____

ANSWERS

A–444

(B)

It is easy to see that the shapes are correct in all the answer choices, so you need to check the point and line positions carefully. Only choice B shows the rectangle's point position accurately. (Line-connector question.) The correct answer is B.

QUESTIONS

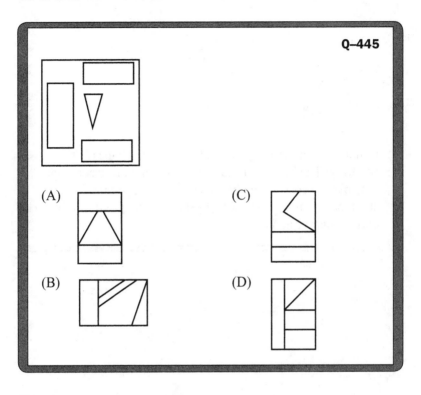

Q-445

(A)

(B)

(C)

(D)

Your Answer _____

ANSWERS

A–445

(A)

Count the number of pieces and check their shapes
carefully! The key to this question is finding an answer that
only has the correct number of correctly shaped pieces—
and there are no odd shapes. (Jigsaw-puzzle question.) The
correct answer is A.

QUESTIONS

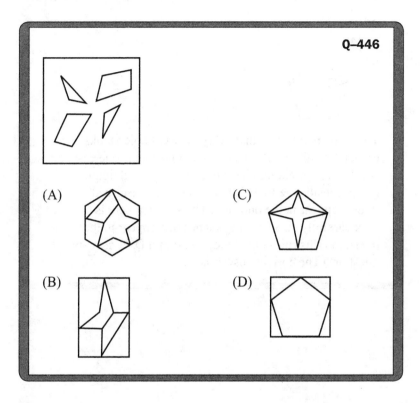

Q–446

(A)

(C)

(B)

(D)

Your Answer _____

ANSWERS

(C)

The challenge here is that every answer choice looks completely different! That actually makes this one easier. All the answer choices have unusual inscribed figures (shapes inside the frame), but none of the inscribed figures appear in the question. The key step here is to look carefully JUST for the shapes that appear in the question. This rules out choices A, B and D. (Jigsaw-puzzle question.) The correct answer is C.

QUESTIONS

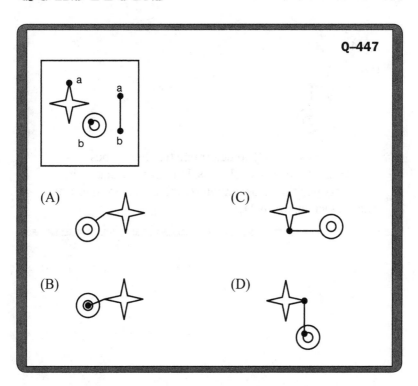

Your Answer _____

ANSWERS

A–447

(D)

You can check quickly to determine that the shapes are correct in all the answer choices, but only one choice has the points positioned accurately. (Line-connector question.) The correct answer is D.

QUESTIONS

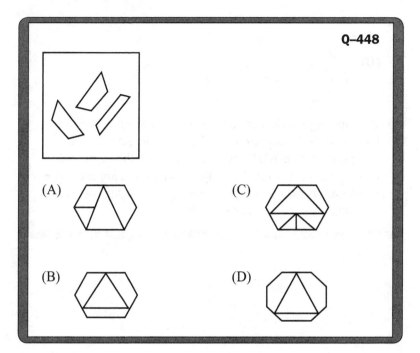

Your Answer _____

_____

ANSWERS

A–448

(B)

By scanning the answer choices, you can see that they all have inscribed triangles (triangle inside the frame)—but the question does NOT have a triangle. So, the key step is to look carefully for and count the shapes that appear in the question. This rules out choices A, C and D. (Jigsaw-puzzle question.) The correct answer is B.

QUESTIONS

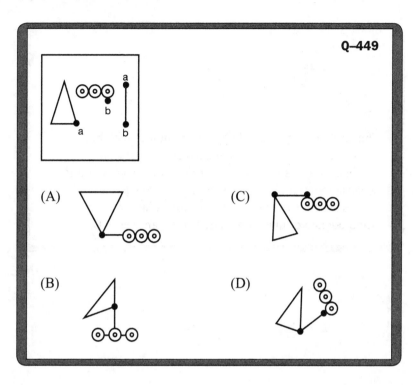

Your Answer _____

ANSWERS

A–449

(D)

This particular question has answer choices with both incorrect shapes, as well as incorrect point placement and line-axis position. You can rule out choices A and B, because the triangles are the wrong shape. Choice C's shapes are fine, but the point position is incorrect. (Line-connector question.) The correct answer is D.

QUESTIONS

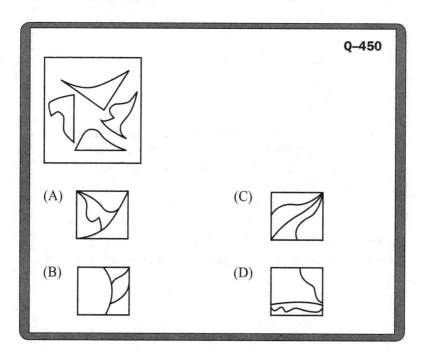

Q–450

(A)

(C)

(B)

(D)

Your Answer _____

ANSWERS

A–450

(A)

These are very distinctive curved pieces, so just check them extra carefully! All the choices have the correct number of pieces, so it is simply a matter of checking for the correct shapes. The two pieces in the question with the most pronounced curves are the easiest ones to look for. If you do, you can rule out choices B, C and D. (Jigsaw-puzzle question.) The correct answer is A.

INSTALLING REA's TestWare®

SYSTEM REQUIREMENTS

Pentium 75 MHz (300 MHz recommended), or a higher or compatible processor; Microsoft Windows® 98 or later, 64 MB RAM; Internet Explorer 5.5 or higher (Internet Explorer 5.5 is included on the CD).

INSTALLATION

1. Insert the ASVAB Flashcard Book TestWare® CD-ROM into the CD-ROM drive.
2. If the installation doesn't begin automatically, from the Start Menu, choose the RUN command. When the RUN dialog box appears, type d:\setup (where *d* is the letter of your CD-ROM drive) at the prompt and click OK.
3. The installation process will begin. A dialog box proposing the directory "Program Files\REA\ASVAB_FC" will appear. If the name and location are suitable, click OK. If you wish to specify a different name or location, type it in and click OK. There are two installation options: Standard and Custom. Standard installation will install all the exams onto your computer. If you only want to install some of the exams, choose Custom Install and follow the instructions.
4. Start the ASVAB Flashcard Book TestWare® application by double-clicking on the icon.

REA's ASVAB Flashcard Book TestWare® is **EASY** to **LEARN AND USE**. To achieve maximum benefits, we recommend that you take a few minutes to go through the on-screen tutorial on your computer. The "screen buttons" are also explained here to familiarize you with the program.

TECHNICAL SUPPORT

REA's TestWare® is backed by customer and technical support. For questions about **installation or operation of your software,** contact us at:

Research & Education Association
Phone: (732) 819-8880 (9 a.m. to 5 p.m. ET, Monday–Friday)
Fax: (732) 819-8808
Website: *www.rea.com*
E-mail: info@rea.com

Note to Windows XP Users: In order for the TestWare® to function properly, please install and run the application under the same computer-administrator level user account. Installing the TestWare® as one user and running it as another could cause file access path conflicts.